a sacred priority.

Sarah

inside

inside

a guide to the resources within

*with 40 self-care practices to
reset, rebalance, and revitalize*

SARAH BRASSARD

Publisher: Jesse Krieger

If you are interested in publishing through Lifestyle Entrepreneurs Press, write to Jesse@LifestyleEntrepreneursPress.com

Publications or foreign rights acquisitions of our catalog books. Learn More: www.LifestyleEntrepreneursPress.com

ISBN 978-1-9466978-6-8

DEDICATION

We all need a foundation of safety and security to grow. For all the loss I endured as I a child, I have only known love, commitment, and devotion from my life with my husband, David. I know a life of healing because of the security and safety you have supplied for me. We have grown together and supported each other through the ebbs and flows, and I am forever grateful to you for the time we have spent together. It is an honor and privilege to dedicate this book to you. Thank you for giving me the chance to trust, love, and live a life so sweet.

ABOUT THE AUTHOR

Sarah Brassard began her professional life as an associate in a high-end fashion boutique before opening her own store in Amherst, New Hampshire, in 1981. In 1990, a year after her second child was born, Sarah sold the store and devoted her life to her young family. It wasn't long before she answered an undeniable calling and began her healing journey by enrolling in the Bancroft School of Massage Therapy. After completing her degree and establishing her practice, Sarah began to educate herself in other healing practices and eventually studied to become a Kundalini yoga instructor, and that spurred her to go to seminary to become an interfaith minister. A spiritual community began to grow around Sarah's healing practices, and at that time she founded a healing center. It was from her work with this community that the inspiration for *Inside* was born. Sarah and her husband, David, split their time between southern New Hampshire and Cape Cod. They have two children, Eric and Alexa, who live in Los Angeles.

CONTENTS

FOREWORD

by Terry Walters, best-selling author of *Clean Food*

Digging deep, listening to our hearts, connecting with our spirit, and being guided by our own personal truth is requisite for good health and a vibrant life. In my own journey, food was the conduit for change. More than understanding the foods that would serve my unique constitution, it was about figuring out how to make positive choices and developing a healthy relationship not only with food but with myself. Over time, my clean food approach influenced my relationships, my connection to the earth and my community, my physical and emotional well-being, and how I moved through the world.

In the beginning I held on with a tight grip, with the rigidity I needed in order to stay the course. Over time, the pieces of my puzzle changed— the food, the environment, my family, and, most importantly, me. When I started, the goal was good health. But as I continued, it became clear that the path I was on was broader. The very same judgments about food that once allowed me to heal were those I needed to let go of in order to grow. The answers that I sought externally for so long I now discovered within. And in learning to trust myself, I was able to embrace a more accepting, more forgiving approach to achieving balance.

Change was the gift that I didn't realize I had received until I stopped and looked back. Developing the ability to connect with mind, body, and spirit is an ongoing challenge that makes it possible to move forward. When we focus on being our best selves, we inspire others to do the same. And the more we breathe this intention out into the world, the sooner the world will start to reflect what is in our hearts.

When we find balance and good health, we are empowered to practice the mindfulness of letting self-love win. The reverse is also true: when we let self-love win, we in turn find balance and good health. It doesn't matter where you start, only *that* you start, and this book provides the inspiration to do so. *Inside* is a catalyst for healing and an empowering guide to vibrant living. With this book, Sarah has crafted a valuable toolbox of practices to help us move authentically in harmony with the expansions and contractions of life. It is a manual for healing body, mind, heart, and spirit that is guaranteed to inspire and change your life for the better. Wise, accessible, heartfelt, useful, and humble, this is a book I will return to often. When we look inside, we find the strength and truth to heal ourselves, and we take the first steps toward healing others, our communities, and our world.

AUTHOR'S NOTE

Dear Reader,

I am writing this note after the completion of the book, and I find myself intrigued with this process of letting it go. This most likely is a familiar experience for a seasoned writer, but I am a newbie in this world of authors. Letting people, places, and things go in my life has always been one of my greatest challenges, and this experience is no different.

Inside is my first book, and it feels like my third child. It is the child that came into my life to help me grow in ways I didn't know I needed to grow. It has helped me know myself and trust my own knowledge. And most importantly, it has given me faith in looking at everything I know and letting it go so I can learn again from that fertile ground of the beginner.

I gifted myself a two-year sabbatical to write this book. It has been one of the hardest things I have ever done. It has required a steady practice of meditation, self-healing, and self-love. I started, like most people questioning my expertise and having to tame and ultimately overcome all the discouragement my mind could throw at me. Believe me, in the beginning, there was a lot of that! But still, I kept on…and it was through that keeping on that I brought this book to completion.

What is keeping on all about? How do we figure out a way to keep on in the midst of hurt, sadness, discouragement, and anger? For me, the most straightforward answer is a strong practice of self-care. It is about becoming the explorer of your inner world. It is finding the power to go inside and excavate the parts of you that feel the most fragile, and that is no small feat. Inner study is the biggest work of our lives, and once accomplished, it will help to lay the foundation for everything else you do in this lifetime.

I am no stranger to the obstacles that can appear on a path of healing. I know all about the best-laid plans and how they can fall flat when a foundation for healing is not in place. This is the reason that I was inspired to write this book. I needed to build a practice of self-healing and ultimately self-love in order to accomplish everything else I needed to do in my life. I had to put a stake in the ground and find my way through the hurt, because the only alternative was regret, anger, and blame for the rest of my life, and that felt like a devastating sacrifice.

As I was writing, at times I would find myself thinking, "Boy, this practice feels like low hanging fruit, so ripe and healing, yet so easy that it's hard to believe it will really work." But it does! And when done with dedication and discipline, these simple practices become a devotional lifestyle that will walk with you for the rest of your life.

I have witnessed in myself and in the many people I have worked with that healing is most effective when, above all, we bring the focus inward and take care of ourselves first. Writing this book has given me that focus in my own life and allowed me to do something I never thought I would be able to do. It offered me the chance to heal through the great losses of my young life and feel the bliss that healing through pain offers. Today I meet you where you are on your path of healing with a deep understanding that wherever you are right now is exactly where you are supposed to be. No matter how hopeless, heartless, or paralyzed you feel in your life, you have opened this book for a reason. Trust that, and open up to the endless possibilities before you.

Sarah

Sarah Brassard
October 2016

INTRODUCTION

Here, at the start of this journey, is a tipping point. Even if it feels like everything's falling apart, and hope and faith feel like words that belong to someone else's vocabulary, right now is a miraculous moment. I know that with certainty because you are seeking. You wouldn't be reading this book if you weren't hoping for a fresh start. You've acknowledged that there is pain in your life, be it physical, mental, emotional, or spiritual. You've and stopped looking for ways to avoid it, disregard it, and run from it. You're now ready to learn how to grow from it and feel better.

On this healing path, are you prepared to look deeper, to reveal and ease your hidden pain and release your sadness? As much discomfort as you feel right now, are you open and willing to explore? It may not feel like it now, but this elevated experience of agitation is your spirit's gift to you. Are you ready to embrace the most fragile aspects of your life and assure them that you are ready to listen, feel, and heal? If so, face your pain and say, "Okay, I am listening, I am ready to experience what hurts most." These unsettled feelings motivate us to learn new ways of being and grow beyond the discomfort.

The walls of resistance come down when we are deeply sad, simply because we don't have the energy to fight anymore. Rather we find ourselves open in this place, not because we have chosen to be here but because life's guidance has brought us here.

It is time to embrace an honest, truthful view of yourself. Once you do, you won't be able to look away, and from that healing view, everything is possible. Emotional walls will be torn down, long-protected reactive feelings will be flushed out, and decisions will be made about the direction of your life. If this feels life changing, believe that feeling and move ahead with determination. Now is the time when the stakes are the highest, and you have a real chance to change the quality of your life for the better. It's up to you. You will be challenged in this book; you can count on that, but alongside those challenges will be nurturing practices that will help you get through whatever comes up.

As we move ahead, I will guide you through gentle and potent shifts that will capture the truest essence of who you are. I will show you how to plant the seeds of self-care, which ultimately will blossom into self-love. The practices in this book are offered to enhance whatever healing protocols, belief systems, or ways of living you already ascribe to. When you have a strong understanding of self-care, you will know that there is no compromising the time we dedicate to ourselves. Not only will you feel improved physical health, but you also will come into relationship with a clear mind, a balanced heart, and a lively spirit. For the first time in a long time, or maybe for the first time ever, you will know what it is like to have your mind, body, heart, and spirit working in harmony with one another. This comes from mastering self-care technology. There is tremendous opportunity for you here, and soon you will recognize your life for what it was always meant to be—happy, whole, peaceful, and blissful. There is no more important work to do than learning to care for and love yourself. With a self-care foundation in place, your life will respond generously, bringing a beautiful ease to your actions.

The work you'll do in this book will help you to receive and be open to the many lessons pain and discomfort offer us when we are strong enough to listen. That is the goal of self-care—to fortify your body, mind, heart, and spirit to meet the ever-changing experiences life delivers to us. With strong self-care practices, you will no longer resist change. These techniques and practices will bring you an awareness that will help you reach for the proper tools when you need them. You will learn how to access your breath as a healing tool. Yoga, meditation, walks in nature, and other rituals will become a part of your life, not as an afterthought but as a necessity and a contributor to your overall strength, courage, and power. I will offer you practices that will help you pay attention to your thoughts, notice your surroundings, and trust your intuition. You'll start to notice how you breathe, how you move, and how you feel in the many scenes of your life. It is in this awakened state that you will live a purposeful and enlightened life.

Self-care is the first step we take on our journey inward. We take our focus, our knowledge, and our compassion and direct it to ourselves. Self-care is the understanding that no sustainable healing can happen without this foundation in place. It is the knowledge that helps us deeply relate to the messages of our body, mind, heart, and spirit so we can become the master translator of these feelings and sensations. When a strong self-care practice is in place, we no longer depend on others to guide our actions. Through our inner study, we learn what makes us happiest and what brings on the most fear, and with this knowledge we cultivate tools to deeply care for the most tender parts of our life.

The first part of the book will focus on the importance of self-care in your life. This will include defining what trauma looks like, creating a relationship with inner peace, and taking ownership of your internal monologue. I will share with you my story of waking up to myself, and even though your journey will be different from mine, my wish is that you will find inspiration from the healing I was able to bring to my life.

In the second part of the book, the emphasis shifts to activity. I will introduce you to the Four Elements—body, mind, heart, and spirit—and we will learn about the qualities of each. You will understand how dependent they are on one another, and that when there is imbalance in one, there are imbalances in the other three. All the elements are connected, just like everything else in our lives, and in gaining this knowledge we broaden our opportunity for growth and happiness. I will guide you through a process of working with each of the elements and then all of them as a whole. The practices included in these chapters are designed to facilitate transformative healing in your life. Then, like parting a dam, doors to strengthen and guide you toward optimal health and well-being will open and you will be ready to process the painful events of the past and welcome in all the possibilities of the future.

Each chapter includes exercises that I refer to as practices, some of which require action, others that take place in the everyday moments of your life. Each one is created for you to remember who you are on the inside, under all that scares you, to awaken your inner knowledge and help you shift out of old habits that no longer work for you. Dedicate yourself to these practices. As simple as they may seem, they will help you learn more about what makes you uniquely you. They will help you cultivate the awareness you need to make big changes, all the while nurturing and fortifying each step you take. Remember to take one step at a time and build your foundation carefully and mindfully so great shifts can happen.

It is not the intention of this book to tell you which spiritual quest is best suited for you but rather to help you build a base, a starting point, and ultimately a foundation strong enough to take on the spiritual journey of your dreams.

You are the true teacher of your life, and each step you take on this self-care journey will bring you closer to your truth. Grow closer to yourself, believe in your ability to change, and watch the arms of your life warmly open to welcome you home once again.

PART
ONE

THE HEALING JOURNEY:

IT STARTS WITH SELF-CARE

Any level of disruption to the body, mind, heart, and spirit leaves an impression, and when we aren't fully aware of that impression, it leaves us dealing with the symptoms of its origin.

Trauma comes in all shapes and sizes. It could be said that we deal with some level of trauma and disruption every day of our lives, but this is not the real crux of what harms and hurts us. The real issue is more than the actual disruption, no matter how big that disruption was. Living with what trauma leaves behind and the disorder it creates in our lives becomes the biggest piece of the puzzle. Many of us who have been affected by trauma are aware of an incident or incidents that have affected us deeply. Having a conscious understanding of what has gone on is the most hopeful of scenarios. The other, more difficult scenario, is that we have closed off our awareness to its presence in our life. While this type of compartmentalization can be a helpful survival technique initially, left unattended it can reap harmful effects on us in the long term.

A lack of awareness is never a positive thing. Awareness is our power; it is our master control system, and when we shut it off, our inner knowledge is limited and we live life functioning on just a few cylinders. Coming back to awareness can invoke all sorts of fear. There is no switch to flip on awareness; it is a gradual process that, as nurtured, will unfurl you. Whatever happened that made you retreat from your feelings needs to be discovered. My experience of growing awareness is that it is very much like peeling the proverbial onion, and this is a consistent and deliberate process. This process is what we will explore in the first part of this book. As you build a life that supports healing at all levels, more information is delivered to you. As you learn how to make time for self-care, you will begin interacting with your life more intimately. You'll no longer feel like you are watching your life from the outside. You will start to ask questions of your inner life, not because you are looking for the right or wrong answer but to gather information so you can observe what's there and heal through it. Anything that is hiding in the dark is difficult to deal with; that is why I have dedicated this part of this book to shedding light on awareness.

It is a natural inclination to run from the pain inside us when it resurfaces to be healed. We take on all sorts of behaviors to avoid what hurts most inside of us. Building a foundation of self-care will support you as your inner pain and the protective walls you've put in place to keep yourself safe are revealed. Self-care will give you the resources to empower every step you take from this point on.

Self-care is the first step in cultivating awareness. It opens you to the whispers inside of you. We retreat when our outer world feels threatened—this is built into our DNA—but how do we undo that threat when it is no longer physically present in our lives? In this part of the book, we will ask this question. We will start our journey together by creating an inner and outer environment that gives us the ability to look inside. Through the self-care practices offered here, you will experience yourself in new ways, through breath, movement, reflection, and nature. I will share with you tools to help you get through difficulty so you no longer have to avoid what has come up to be healed but rather boldly welcome it.

We will look at the many different ways trauma presents and work toward a clear view of how it has manifested for each of us in our lives. You will learn to consult your inner knowledge before searching outside of yourself. By looking inward, you honor yourself in a different way than ever before. You will learn how to change old habits and become open to the many possibilities that exist in your life. You will get stronger, more compassionate, and more forgiving, and in offering this gift to yourself, others will understand how to take care of you, and you will have the ability to offer this gift to the world as well.

We are all different, and it is these differences that make us so magnificent. A foundation of self-care helps you to know the truth about your life and gives others the chance to learn who you truly are. This is an honest path, no more games to play, no more drama to negotiate, just a clear and truthful understanding of what you can do and what you choose not to do. Self-care opens a dialogue with the most precious parts of who we are inside. It all starts here.

chapter *1*

Become the Explorer
of Your Inner World

There is no greater gift than the time we spend getting to know ourselves: our joys, our quirky habits, and the tender places in our hearts that get triggered by life around us. Why is self-knowledge so important? Because it builds a foundation for self-love—one that is strong, resilient, and efficient at taking care of us. When self-love falls into place, we begin to trust our ability to deal with whatever comes up for us in life. Situations and circumstances that used to disrupt our energy no longer do so. The effects of truly knowing ourselves are profound, and soon we are living a life we never thought possible.

There is so much we can discover when we clear the way and listen to who we are on the inside. If this sounds like a new language to you, trust that you'll know it soon. You'll understand that all the messages you are given, whether they come from physical discomfort, emotional upset, or a spiritual crisis, have come to you for a reason. This is the language of your inner world. This book has come into your life as a tool to help you translate these messages. It is through that translation that you will grow strong enough to move through the challenging events of life and come out more powerful on the other side.

Follow the intrigue of your inquiry to heal, and trust that you are on the path you need to be on, even if that path feels like the rockiest and steepest path of all. Wherever you are right now is exactly where you are supposed to be. It takes all sorts of circumstances to motivate us to look at life in a fresh and promising new way. So rather than judge the conditions of your life, bring awareness to them. Recognize the magnitude of your feelings and do your best to not get stuck there. As we will learn, the only way through discomfort and suffering is straight through it. Cherish the fact that you are feeling anything, even if those feelings are bringing you tremendous discomfort. It is better than the alternative of not feeling at all, and it is the first step on your path to healing.

We avoid inner pain for good reason: when we are not strong enough to look at our greatest fears, we do everything we can to get away from that which frightens us most. This might help you avoid the hurt for a while, but soon it returns. Our pain comes into our awareness to be healed, and until we can do that, it will come back again and again, gaining strength and disrupting our lives each time. It takes strength and courage to move through it, but the alternative is spending a lifetime trying to outrun it and ultimately only reinforcing the pain. Healing our lives takes a strong commitment to moving past our most difficult experiences. Until we do this, we are stuck living within the limitations of pain.

When we commit to making changes, we become the explorers of our inner world. Just like any conquest, we gain more knowledge of who we are and what it takes to thrive in the world around us. We are adventurers, ready and willing to take on all obstacles. Change no longer frightens us because we are ready for the lessons we'll learn along the way, and each time we learn, we grow stronger. When we find the ability to grow rather than get stuck, we can hold dear the many experiences of a great life.

OPENING YOURSELF UP TO SELF-HEALING

Self-healing means acting from a place of compassion for the body, mind, heart, and spirit. It is a gentle, nurturing relationship with your own needs that is a vital part of building a happy and fulfilled life. Shouldn't self-healing be a given, an innate part of how we take care of ourselves? The reality is that self-healing can actually be quite difficult to put into place.

Too often compassion for ourselves gets lost through the many unresolved issues we accumulate over the years, and self-healing becomes an unfeasible goal, or even a seemingly selfish one. With every sadness we harbor or angry feeling we suppress, we move further and further away from the love of self. This disconnection takes away our ability to be our authentic selves, who we truly are. On the flipside, when we nurture ourselves with self-healing, it becomes our inner guiding force and makes us into strong, generous people, ready to give more to our loved ones and communities, ready to stand up for what we believe in, and ready to put our energy into our life's work.

Welcome to the gentle beginning of your journey to inner healing. This path of learning takes your focus from the outer circumstances of life and draws you inward. Inside, you have the wisdom to heal through the most difficult parts of life and to prepare for a future of great joy. The challenges ahead require that we come into deep relationship with who we are. What is it that beats our hearts, makes us sing with joy, and nurtures the beautiful life we have been given?

STARTING WITH SELF-CARE

Self-care is a method of wellness that focuses on nurturing yourself so that you can be healthier in your body and mind, happier in your life, and a better loved one to those you care about. Self-care is about trusting yourself, being aware of your needs, and knowing intimately what makes you safest and most secure. When we build our life's foundation on self-care, we have the tremendous capacity to help others do the same.

Throughout this book, I will guide you through simple self-care practices that combine ancient techniques and cutting-edge wellness systems to build a foundation of self-healing. The more you practice them, the more you will notice their value in relation to everything else you do. Through deep listening, you will gain information about your sensitivities, what makes you feel strong and inspired, and what leaves you feeling drained and motionless. Self-care is a window into your life, and with a curious eye you will gain expertise on who you are, and that will serve you for the rest of your life. With each act of self-care, large or small, you gain invaluable personal knowledge. You direct your energy and focus inward, first, and from there, you fortify and balance your sense of self.

When you are not paying attention to your life as a whole, you can overlook subtle warning signs to address your body, mind, heart, and spirit. With a conscious awareness, you tend to these issues before they become a greater concern. Self-care offers an introspective view of the whole rather than the narrow, restricted view that comes from a stress-oriented perspective. When you are able to see a potentially harmful situation before it affects your life adversely, there are abundant opportunities to heal.

I have dedicated my career to helping people understand how to reset, revitalize, and rebalance themselves after trauma. Listen to the messages of your life with a deeply compassionate and empathetic ear and watch how your life responds. Self-care opens a dialogue with the most precious parts of who you are inside. Your inner world is vulnerable to deep pain from traumas of the past, and when the pain is most intense, it is tempting to want to move away from it or ignore it. Though it might seem easier to block off the feelings, even in a state of pain, your inner self holds the answers to your search for direction.

When self-care is in place, healing can begin. You figure out how best to support your well-being and keep a close eye on your health and happiness. You know at all times which parts of your life are thriving and which parts are in need of support. Self-care practices and a respectful inner dialogue will help you gather valuable information about who you are, and this becomes a starting place for how you interact with your life. It takes consistent attention and courage to persevere, but it will be the most precious asset you can ever give yourself.

When I earnestly brought self-care practices into my life, I noticed space open up in my life. I had never realized how much room my fear, sadness, and anxiety took up. I would wake up anxious about the day ahead, and all I could see were obstacles and challenges; it was hard to do much else other than manage them. When you start to feel your burden of fear release, you may find yourself doing something spontaneous and unexpected. This could be something big like booking a flight when your fear of flying has kept you from traveling by plane your whole life or as simple as taking a longer route home just to take in the scenery. Self-care opens us up to a part of our spirit that we cannot access in a state of fear, and it motivates us to learn and grow further.

YOU ARE THE EXPERT ON YOU

So often we don't believe in our own power. We lose touch with that part of ourselves that believes we have the ability to change the way life looks. We leave ourselves out of our healing equation and hand our power off to someone else: a doctor, therapist, teacher, parent, friend, lover, or colleague. We count on them to tell us what is going on in our lives because we don't know or trust ourselves enough to figure it out. It's an easier route, initially, than having to dig in and heal your life from the inside out. But this is a slippery slope. The feedback we get from those around us is incredibly valuable, but not when we haven't developed an understanding of who we are first. When we are out of touch with our personal health or our mental and spiritual well-being, the scales of life tip and it's hard to gauge what's real for us. We are looking at our life through someone else's lens, and this is a confusing perspective. In this place, our view becomes tainted by the circumstances of life, and before long we trust our outer world more than we trust our own inner knowledge of who we are and what we need to be happy and healthy in our lives.

It is easy to understand how this happens. Imbalance occurs when we devote more time to interacting with our outer world than we do listening to the inner callings of what we have come here to do. Inevitably, we have lost our way and become discouraged by the challenges that have been placed before us. This is why this inner work is so important. Everything we do in an effort to strengthen our personal relationship with ourselves will fortify us. There will be a day when we will meet sadness, loss, sickness, and weakness; this is the reality of being a human being. We are not here forever. We too will leave this world someday, and the sooner we embrace that reality, the sooner we can start really living. Knowing ourselves deeply allows us to live fully; this is something that's especially important as we age but invaluable at all points in our lives.

No one will ever know you as well as you know yourself, and no one will ever be able to heal your physical, emotional, and spiritual wounds as well as you can. You are the expert on you. But it takes time, discipline, and a deep yearning for change. If you are really listening, you'll hear the callings of your soul. It is these callings that prompt us toward the true purpose of our life and will draw the appropriate healers to us. But when ignored, these inner callings soon become demanding and create a disruption that is hard to ignore.

In life there is no more important job than to learn about the intricacies of who you are. From this place your personal lens will become clear so you can navigate life's events with an assurance and faith that did not exist before. You will have knowledge of your life that no one else does, and this will increase your opportunities for sustaining a lifelong path of healing and happiness.

FINDING A NEW RELATIONSHIP WITH PAIN

When I talk about trauma, loss, or pain, I'm pointing to experiences that leave an imprint on our lives and continue to affect us for months or years after the event is over. In my own life, significant changes happened when I came to know that pain was not the enemy. I ran from pain for years; it wasn't until I finally accepted pain as a teacher that I could know health and happiness.

Moving *away* from pain isn't the same as moving through pain. You can run from pain until you're exhausted, but your pain will always find you. You can wear a mask to shield yourself from pain, but pain will always recognize you. When you at last stand face to face with what hurts you most and frightens you to the core, an amazing thing happens: pain asks to be released, and you begin to feel it loosen its grip on your life. Living with the imprint of pain every minute of every day is a limiting way to exist. You deserve better than to accept this sad, hopeless state.

I wish that I could tell you, "I saw pain as my teacher and then *everything* changed!" But the truth is, my life got better incrementally. As I gained an awareness of the need to heal myself first, before I addressed the greater issues of my life, so much shifted for me. It's easy to want to look for that one big miracle. I certainly can relate to that longing, but I know better now. For most of us, hard work and consistency are the miracle. It starts with deciding not to live in suffering anymore, and from there patience, grace, openness, and love usher in a new way of being in the world.

CONNECTING TO YOUR ENERGETIC SELF

How do you gauge whether you feel strong or tired? You measure your energy level. How do you express your enthusiasm over something? With energetic responses. How do you describe the personality of someone you meet? By the energy their personality generates. Many of us may only interact with our energy in the most obvious times, but true wellness means honoring your energy as your life force.

We are energetic beings, and the energy of life is something we all have a relationship with, whether we pay attention to it or not. Energy is the glue that binds the body, mind, heart, and spirit and is the flowing source of vitality in life.

Many of us mismanage our energy unconsciously by not paying enough attention to our energy levels until we are burned out and in disaster mode. Fear, sadness, anxiety, and other roadblocks get in the way of the healing flow. Until you honor and tend to the amazing force of energy, you will lose out on one of the greatest healing tools available to you.

Energy healing is a very practical science that can swiftly improve your quality of life, and the promising news is that there are so many ancient practices and modern techniques available to us that can put us back in touch with our inner nature. Through a steady self-care regime, you will soon come back into relationship with your energetic health. You'll understand when your energy flows freely and when it does not. With diligence and commitment, you can reestablish the connection to your energy and feel its abundant healing gifts. You will begin to pay attention to yourself—not sometimes, but all the time. You will focus on what you eat, create, think, and feel. You will begin to recognize what charges you up and what drains you.

The vitality of life exists in the balance and energy flow of the body, mind, heart, and spirit. On any given day, the difference between success and failure can depend on your energy level and your ability to be at your best. The practices in this book are designed to balance and energize your energetic system so you can cultivate more vitality in your life. Once you make the commitment, the universe will support you in astounding ways.

THANK THE DISCOMFORT AND START FRESH

You have now been introduced to pain as your teacher. There is no denying that this perspective can feel challenging and calls you to open your mind, heart, and spirit to new ways of being in the world. It is also perfectly acceptable to acknowledge that you're not ready for that level of learning yet. Be assured that I have taken that into consideration. I am introducing you to these new concepts and practices slowly, but always know that there is no greater teacher to your inner experience than you are to yourself.

Healing and growing is a balancing act of moving toward your edge and slowing the pace down when life feels too scary or frightening. Listen to the messages of resistance that your body, mind, heart, and spirit send to you. That is where all the information for healing resides. Don't push yourself too far and risk feeling unsafe. Slowing down isn't failing. It's a demonstration of self-love and self-care. Finding balance will help you keep going. Don't give up! You are still making progress, and little by little, you will move through painful obstacles.

When people quit, it's not because quitting feels good. *Healing* feels good. The problem is that healing takes a committed path of continuing on, no matter what obstacles appear, and that can be really hard. People give up because they haven't had the chance to cultivate the strength it takes to do this level of inner work; they didn't have their energetic foundation in place. This type of deep healing is not for the faint of heart. Sometimes it takes daunting suffering and nagging dissatisfaction to wake us up to what hurts so very much. But when we finally understand that what hurts most is not to be ignored but listened to, we find the courage and ability to heal. We commit to transforming our suffering and making it into the most potent teacher of our life. We find that the more difficult the situation is, the more potency there is in the lesson it's teaching us.

The days and weeks ahead will be different from the many times before when you said you would change and didn't. Even now, just these few pages in, you have begun to think about the interconnectedness of your body, mind, heart, and spirit. You have thought about what energy means to your life by measuring your energy level. The changes have already begun and the journey is underway.

PRACTICE: GROUNDING

There are all sorts of situations that have the potential to unglue us. When we pay close attention to our life, we find that along with abundant joy there are situations that have the potential to make us feel very uncomfortable. This is life. It is made up of both. When we can accept this, we find the tools we need to stay present to what appears. Simply asking the question, "How did this situation make me feel?" activates self-care.

Grounding practices plant us firmly in the power of our life. In this one, I ask you to notice yourself not as a victim of the circumstances around you but as a powerful contributor. We always have a choice. When we cultivate tools to take care of the feelings that show up, we build a powerful base that responds generously to the world around us. Use this technique when a situation or interaction with someone leaves you feeling sad, confused, angry, anxious, or resentful.

— TO DO THE PRACTICE —

1 Sit on a chair or in a comfy, supported seat on the floor and breathe into your connection to the earth. Feel the energetic contact and imagine roots growing deeply into the earth from the base of your spine or feet. Breathe into these roots and visualize them going deep and wide into the ground. Spend as much time here as you need to in order to feel fully supported.

2 Ask yourself, "How did this situation make me feel?"

3 If there is negativity in your answer, rather than digging in further to what might be going on, simply offer yourself the chance to feel grounded and safe through your connection to the earth in this moment.

EMBARK ON A JOURNALING PRACTICE

I have been journaling since I was twelve years old. I have no recollection of how I was inspired to start, but I have a very clear memory of how journaling helped me release the intensity of my emotions so I could carry on with my day. My journaling practice helped me reflect on rather than deflect the impactful events of my life. Had I not had this outlet, there are times when I would have been immobilized. By witnessing my thoughts and feelings on the page, journaling helped me process my confusion and anger in a healthy manner. I named my journal ETC., and I wrote volumes in my early life.

The power of putting pen to paper is storied, and the how-to is simple: write it down. The most effective journaling is a mirror, a release valve, and a vision board. It's a medium without judgment because the only audience for your journal will be you. It has been through journaling that I have become my own best teacher.

There's a very specific kind of relief that comes from writing down your feelings and unloading worry and concern. Sometimes releasing feelings by talking it out or working it out does the trick. But journaling serves as both a release and a sounding board. My relationship with journaling is deep and personal, and my hope is that it will be for you too.

There are no points for style or grammar when you journal. You've already succeeded by picking up the pen; from there everything that you put on paper will serve you without exception. Modern technology has offered us countless ways to journal, and no one method is better than another. Here are a few of my favorites:

* Go to a bookstore and buy a journal and pen that appeal to you
* Send your journal entry in an e-mail to yourself
* Record yourself in a voice memo on your phone

In the pages ahead, you will be asked to record your feelings in your journal with a goal of unearthing valuable information about yourself. With a dedicated journaling practice, you will be able to reflect on the changes that arise from the simple act of looking inside.

PRACTICE: JOURNALING

Journaling is a tool that helps us unearth emotions that might not be accessible in our day-to-day consciousness but still strongly affect everything we do. Journaling has helped me dig deeper into who I am, bringing to light my likes and dislikes, my fears and my joys. I have been truly astonished by what journaling has revealed to me. The following are two exercises to get you started. They are designed to help tease out knowledge about who you are at a very deep level. Whatever emotions show up, do your best to welcome them.

1. Being Grateful

First thing in the morning, open your journal and write down three things that you're grateful for. It can be anything you want it to be; it is for your eyes only. These are some examples of things I am grateful for in my life:

* My relationship with God, the universe, and nature
* Living close to a hiking trail
* Fresh air
* The seashore
* Comfy sheets and blankets
* Manicures/pedicures
* My garden
* Summer parties on the deck

2. Letting It Out

For this practice, simply make note of what's on your mind. For example:

* "I keep getting distracted when my boss puts me on the spot."
* "I'm so fat. I can't say no to cheesecake."
* "I miss him/her. I'm so lonely."

The most frank statements are the easiest to address. You may find that they are also the hardest to write. I encourage you to practice writing these sorts of statements:

* "I don't like the way he spoke to me."
* "I'd like to learn to be a better cook."
* "My father-in-law gets on my nerves."

Or simply unwind. For example:

* "That made me so mad I couldn't see straight. Who does she think she is?"
* "I had to get out of there. I felt like the walls were closing in on me."
* "It was amazing, he made me feel like the only person in the room!"

As you do this exercise, you're not looking for profundity. You're looking for truth, your truth. Spend as much time as you need—keep writing until you've let it all out!

PRACTICE: CREATING A VISION BOARD

A vision board is where your thoughts become actions. First you put your vision on paper. It can be about anything. Then build on what appears and continue to write about it. Dream big, indulge yourself in thoughts of love and growth, and visualize what it will feel like when your vision is realized. Be specific and positive here. Put it out there!

Here are some examples:

* "Within three months I'm going to run three miles without stopping."
* "I will meet the person I share my life with."
* "I'm going to get that job."

Continue to build on your vision board and revisit it periodically as you work through the practices in the book. That way you can chart your progress and continue to grow in new and unexpected ways.

chapter 2

Waking Up to Myself

- -

ILLUMINATION

The events that made the biggest impression on my life happened long ago. Four decades back, my mother left our family and my father died shortly thereafter from complications of leukemia. The details of the story and the reasons why things happened as they did are no longer what's most important. What feels far more essential and life-affirming is that I made it through the anger, bitterness, blame, and feelings of abandonment. I healed through the desperate emotions that sat in the forefront of my life triggering my thoughts and actions.

After the losses, I sheltered myself from the hurt, blocking off the natural flow of feelings that were asking for healing. I spent my teenage and young adult years in the discomfort of managing those feelings. I felt the weight and destruction they brought to my life and, without the strength to look at them, I wallowed in the victimhood and sadness they brought to my life. This was the way I lived for a long time until at last these emotions woke me up to the misery I was feeling. I could no longer bear the dead end road of unsuccessful attempts at changing. I was ready to find the strength to change the course of my life. I became motivated to release the grip that suffering had on me. I knew there was more to life than the narrow, restricted hurt I was feeling, and as soon as I understood that, my world opened up and the healing began.

What I have come to learn and respect about the direction of my life is that there are no mistakes. Life happens just as it is meant to happen. The good, the bad, and the ugly happen for each of us in their own shape and form.

We are all unique in how we respond to life's events. What hurts and harms one person may be a nonissue for someone else. We each have our individual sensitivities, and once we know what they are, we have the ability to know how to relate to them. We can find tools to help us heal what needs to be healed. We no longer judge whether or not these feelings are worthy of healing. When they show up, they are there to be healed.

I ran from my feelings for a long time, always with the same discouraging results. My suffering served me, though, because every time I hurt, I recognized the discomfort as the next great chance to look deeper into who I was, and it nudged me toward healing. I discovered that the tools I had used to stay afloat from the losses of my childhood had made me stronger. I had become someone who dealt with adversity well. It was a challenging path, but as the sad imprints healed and life's suffering let go, what remained was my strength and tenacity. This is what I draw on now. I am no longer a victim of my life.

Now, even in my most challenging moments, I know how to make myself feel better. Sometimes better is a real turnaround, and other times it means knowing how to hold steady through long-term difficulties. I have a foundation that is equipped to deal with whatever shows up. My practices didn't take away the trauma in my life; that wouldn't be real life. What they did do was give me the strength and comfort to deal with the many variable outer circumstances of my life. Instead of shutting down or avoiding difficulty now, I have the chance to meet it and say yes, I am ready to heal and do what needs to be done.

I no longer fear the reorganization of change. My energy's vitality isn't dependent on the conditions that exist outside my life. I have built strength and structure from the inside out. When challenges present, I don't look to adjust or manipulate my outer conditions. I go inside first. This has been the great value of my meditation, yoga, and other self-care practices. For every moment I give to my practices, I learn and grow in abundant ways. I have precious information about my mind, body, heart, and spirit. I know how to nurture them so they can support this life I have come here to live. With this foundation I continue, each day, to build my inner life.

BUILDING LIFE ON A FOUNDATION OF PAIN

As a teenager and young adult, I spent my life coping with the difficulty of panic attacks, relationship confrontations, emotional highs and lows, and back again. Anxiety, a stream of adrenaline that drove me forward through the numbness, was what kept me going. Getting through life as an anxious person did not seem destructive to me at the time. I could stay in control of my life through the pain and drama, although sooner or later I would find myself trapped in the same old terrifying issues times ten. I had become so familiar with panic attacks that it was hard to separate reality from trauma. What I came to understand was that anything could trigger the emotions and sensations, and without any awareness of the root of the feelings, I was left feeling even more helpless and frightened.

I got married in my twenties, and witnessing these rapid changes confused and worried my husband. He wanted me to get well, but we had no idea where to start. Was it a physical condition? Or did I need to talk to a psychologist? We had so many questions and very few answers.

This is the thing with trauma: it often creeps in through the back door unannounced, with no explanation, to wreak havoc on your life. It was not until I changed the direction of my efforts and moved inward, through therapy, meditation, and other self-care practices that encouraged the reconnection to my inner self, that I began to figure out what would ultimately heal me.

What amazes me now is how long I coped in this way. On top of all those unhealthy coping skills, I had a tremendous need for things to look perfect to hide how empty I felt inside. So I carried on with the exhausting anxiety issues, the depleting coping mechanisms, and the building of a facade that wasn't me, until one day when my body slammed me to the ground with a severe case of pneumonia. I was unable to do anything but stay in bed for two weeks. The blessing of this illness was that it gave me the time I so desperately needed to reflect and reset my life on a healing journey.

I knew things had to change, but with so much to do—taking care of our six-month-old son and owning and running a clothing business—how was I going to accomplish that? What became clear to me in that two-week recovery was that I had no choice. If life kept up this way, I was going to simmer in unhappiness, disease, and disruption for the rest of my life. This realization scared the hell out of me. Something had to change.

Earlier that fall, my husband, David, our young son, Eric, and I went to stay at a beach house on the north shore of Massachusetts. Anxiety attacks put my system on high alert, and I can remember the details like it was yesterday instead of twenty-eight years ago.

That night, David drove off to pick up pizza for dinner. An hour later, he still had not come home. This was in the days when cell phones were not a part of life, and I had been keeping track of the time since he left. I managed to ward off my concerns for a half hour after his expected arrival time had come and gone, but when an hour passed, I went into a full-blown panic attack. My mind raced. I imagined calling the police and finding out about a fatal crash. I was planning David's funeral. I envisioned our child growing up without a father. I was stranded on this island with a baby and no car, overcome in a tunnel of terror—which is what my panic attacks so often felt like—when he arrived home with dinner. It was a busy night at the pizza place, and he didn't think twice about waiting the extra forty-five minutes.

I was exhausted and angry. *Where had he been, and did he know what I had gone through?* Of course he didn't. David was blown away by my fear. He couldn't imagine what had happened to me to warrant this kind of reaction. I was just as confused and shocked myself, and I struggled to get any words out to help him understand. Our two realities couldn't have been more divided.

What this situation taught me was that there was no stuffing my trauma, anxiety, and panic away. Thankfully, I realized that the pain was looking for a way out, not to ruin my life, but to *heal* it.

REAWAKENING MY INNER CHILD

In the losses of my young life, my inner child, the person I was when I was born, went away. That tender, trusting, open child was no longer a part of who I was. I couldn't remember what it was like to have faith, to be spontaneous, and to be free from the burdens of fear. The habits I took on to get through the losses were rigid, controlled, and guarded. I became hypervigilant in my actions, prepared for the next ball to drop. I understand this now, but I didn't then. I didn't sit around wondering where my inner child had gone. I didn't even remember that once I'd had the innocence of a young child. The information I could access was the family structure I had known for the first ten years of my life, followed by the loss of my parents. I had memories of the love and connection we had all shared, but it faded fast with the loss. This is the tragedy of trauma, and it was one of the most challenging parts of my recovery from loss and abandonment. I remembered little of what life had felt like before the trauma. There was happiness once, but now, still weighted with anger, blame, and hurt, I had a hard time finding the joy that existed in the past.

The personal circumstances of your life that have brought you to this book may be very different from this abbreviated version of my story, but still I am sure you can relate to the impact. We are kindred in that way. The facts are what they are with trauma, and awareness of trauma is the most potent way to heal through it. When we spend too much time reliving the event and not dealing with the symptoms, we head in a less productive direction. These events are not the story; they are just the start of the story. For me the events pushed me from one path—a predictable, comfortable, and sheltered one—onto another steeper and more rugged one, filled with opportunity for growing, learning, and eventual healing.

This is healing in its most precious expression. When we have cultivated the strength to transform our sad story into an inspiring story, one of empowerment and compassion, we help others know hope through us. It is this type of healing that encourages us to reawaken, to come out from under the protective walls that at one time may have helped us cope but no longer help us grow. Then the inner child is encouraged to take part in our lives once again and life begins to flow in an unrestricted way.

UNDERSTANDING SUFFERING'S GIFTS

My survival methods made me a very productive person for many years. I built a mask of perfection around my life. I founded a business at twenty-one and ran the company for ten years. I met the man of my dreams at twenty-two and married him at twenty-five. I had our first child at twenty-six and our second child at twenty-nine, a boy and girl respectively. We bought our first house in a beautiful community in southern New Hampshire, and before I was thirty I had all of what most people dream of having in a lifetime. But despite all this, the cracks were appearing, and I couldn't seal them up fast enough.

Yes, you can be in pain and still function in normal life. You can be successful while still struggling with deep feelings of fear, grief, inadequacy, anger, and self-hate. You can spend every day doing what others tell you is right and important, but that won't heal your life. When you stop, really stop, and reflect on how life feels for you in this moment, then you have an honest starting point.

Suffering motivated me to change. I was getting increasingly tired of managing the symptoms of my insecurities. My world was shrinking because my fears were growing stronger and accelerating, and on this track there was nothing in my future that looked different from that. I needed a big shift in my outlook.

In my most desperate times, I was driven by my anguish and fear. I moved at a fast pace, making plans for my family, organizing social events, working to further my career. This helped me keep my unsettled feelings at bay. I have always had a strong intuition, but at this point in time my intuition was a hindrance to me. It called me to heal, but I was not ready. I was still too stuck in anger and the management of that anger. I chose not to look deeper than the symptoms of my sadness. If something made me sad, I ran from it. I was getting in touch with how much my life hurt, but I had not yet reached a point where I was strong enough or motivated enough to do something about it.

Suffering supplies us with everything we need to heal, but if we are not in a place that recognizes that the suffering is even there, it's hard to find the deeper meaning. Healing through emotional disruption requires that we first understand how trauma has impacted our life. Sometimes we have to sit in suffering for a long time—like I did—and other times it moves through more quickly.

Suffering was my opportunity, guide, and messenger. It made me stronger and more capable of dealing with adversity. I am not sure I understood suffering's gift then, but now I do. I had to change the way I looked at my life to find the strength to believe again. To excavate the glimmer of hope that was still alive in me under all the suffering took courage. I had to build a foundation of courage first before I could move ahead with my healing. How could this young, closed-hearted, fiercely protected, reactive little girl get what she needed to move ahead as a balanced, successful, and joyful adult?

Intentions can move mountains. I was very familiar with the long-told story of my life. What I was less familiar with was how I was going to heal through it. For me it started with the simple decision to do something different from what I had done before.

LISTENING TO MY BODY

The fear inside of me affected my decisions, my emotional well-being, and eventually my physical health. Many people can guide themselves to healing before emotional, mental, and spiritual energy manifests disease to the body. But in my case, it was my physical conditions that woke me up to the disease that lived in my spirit and propelled me to make changes.

During this time of disorder I was constantly ridden with colds, allergies, and flu. My immune system was compromised. I was coming down with physical ailments that were not typical of a healthy young woman. The breaking point for me was when I became critically ill with pneumonia and then shingles. My world stopped. I was young, yet I felt quite old. While my body was trying to heal, my spirit was sluggish and discouraged. This was a supremely challenging time. Now, not only was I physically unable to move away from my suffering, but my hidden emotional pain—my grief, anger, resistance, and negativity—showed up too. My heart was hurting, and now it laid heavily on my spirit, body, and mind too. My years of hiding behind a mask were coming to an end. I couldn't pretend anymore. The physical symptoms could no longer be avoided, and I needed to face what was showing up.

My body is my teacher. When I don't understand the messages from my mind and I can't relate to the yearnings of my heart, I have disconnected from the spirit's wisdom. That's when my body grabs ahold of me. It shakes me awake through physical symptoms to tell me I cannot move away from this discomfort any longer. I need to stay still and heal. No longer able to outrun the discomfort, I had no choice but to stay with it and heal through it. The blessing of this story is that this time I listened. I knew that if I didn't start paying attention to my physical afflictions, I would grow increasingly more fragile and susceptible to disease. Thus began my healing journey.

Looking back, this uncomfortable period was the greatest opportunity of my life. My young coping methods had worked for a long time but had now run their course and were wearing me down. The grief that hid under the surface of my life was bubbling up to be seen, heard, and released. Gone were the days when I could superficially dust off discomfort. It was time to lift up the furniture in my life and do a thorough spring cleaning. It was this turning point that launched me into a deeper path of seeking and learning and propelled my life in another direction.

RELEASING BLAME, ACCEPTING RESPONSIBILITY

One of the most challenging things for me to heal through was blame. In my most fragile times, I placed blame and responsibility on others for my difficulties and would fall victim to what was going on around me. My life felt like an ongoing battle. Difficult stuff kept showing up, and all I could do was push it away. At that time I had no understanding of what it took to release myself from this ineffective cycle of hurt, so I kept my feelings as far from my heart as possible.

I can remember the first time I learned about personal ownership. I was taking a course at a yoga studio on the *Bhagavad Gita*, a famous Hindu scripture on spirituality. The teacher, a woman I had come to trust, opened by saying that there are no mistakes in life, and *everything* happens for a reason. These words set my brain spinning. Instantly my mind rejected them, interrupting the lesson with all of the exceptions and loopholes that applied to my unique case. But my spirit urged me to listen. Even though my mind was protesting, the deep message of this text was speaking directly to my soul. I knew something important was happening, so I listened. According to the *Bhagavad Gita,* she explained, each lifetime is a chance for the soul to learn, and that learning only exists when we are open, loving, and forgiving. No learning happens when we are stuck in hatred, victimhood, or anger. Now this I could relate to. I knew intuitively the discomfort I felt in my body, mind, heart, and spirit when I repeated cycles of suffering. I wasn't learning, and my pain had stopped me from growing.

The *Bhagavad Gita*'s concept of the evolution of the soul sparked something deep within me. What if I had a choice? What if I could actually learn a new way of being that would help me grow out of old triggers, hurts, and reactions just by staying open instead of closing down from the pain? This text appeared to be offering me a new course for my life, and I was willing to give it a try.

TAKING OWNERSHIP OF MY LIFE

When we take inventory of our lives, we become empowered. We have the chance to start fresh. No one else holds any of our cards; we call all the shots in our healing. I started implementing change by owning everything in my life—the good, the bad, and the ugly—it was all mine to digest and take responsibility for.

Ownership motivated me to look deeper into the hurt that was holding me back. I had spent enough time feeling emotionally unsuccessful, and now I was ready to make a change. Life moves on, not with our instructions but with a universal script that happens, for the most part, out of our control. What we *can* decide on and act upon, though, is the way we respond to what shows up. Do we shut down, complain, forever feel the victim? Or do we cultivate a life that is resilient enough to deal with the most difficult events with grace? I chose the latter, not as a heroic move, but initially for self-preservation, and then later to facilitate deeper inner growth.

I think globally now, no longer stuck in the tiny world of fear that used to define my life. I take delicate care of my vessel—body, mind, heart, and spirit—and have a discerning eye in how I relate to my environment. I began to see how my day-to-day complaints were merely informative memos on how to better tend to myself in that moment, not detailed summaries of doom. I started thinking in terms of my greater self—not the person who was born on a certain date in this lifetime, but as a soul that had journeyed for many lifetimes in hopes of healing just that much more each time.

As I went about implementing these shifts, I needed constant reminders to keep me on course, and the healing practices in this book are those very reminders. The Safe Haven practice is one I turn to to prevent old feelings and behaviors from sneaking back in.

PRACTICE: SAFE HAVEN

Fear puts a blanket over all that makes us feel safe and secure. This practice puts us back in relationship with that security and gives us the courage to take the next steps needed to heal. Think of it as a hopeful starting point, a place you can return to when your healing path becomes challenging and less clear. When we have security—through the love of another person, a physical location, or a place in our mind that soothes us—we have a valuable tool to move ahead and meet whatever challenges appear.

After the loss of my parents, everything changed for me. There was an estrangement from the most familiar parts of my life, and I was left feeling very unsafe. This loss invoked tremendous fear in me. I was challenged to find something that offered me security. When I came across this simple practice, it not only helped me feel safe in my environment; it also encouraged me to look more deeply into my sadness and fears.

You may have a reference point for safety and security that you can build on (for me it is a wooded knoll on Cape Cod that overlooks the bay), or you may need to spend time creating one. Be patient—it will come, and when it does, it will help you to create a foundation for the work ahead. You might try picking up a magazine and flipping through the pages. Notice how various pictures make you feel. When you find a picture that makes you feel at home, happy, and peaceful, remember it and use it for this practice.

— TO DO THE PRACTICE —

1 Find a quiet place in your home. Sit on a chair or a supported seat on the floor. (If you are on a chair, make sure your feet can touch the ground.)

2 Lengthen your spine and take three deep breaths.

3 Visualize your breath coming in from the ground below you.

4 Feel yourself drink in the energy of the earth through your feet. (If you are on the ground, feel this same energy come through all parts of your body that touch the ground.)

5 Now close your eyes and visualize in your mind's eye a place that brings you comfort.

6 With your eyes closed, pay attention to the details of your safe haven. Allow this experience to be all yours. Let your imagination grow your safe haven's beauty, and blanket yourself in it. Notice:

+ The color of the sky

+ The temperature of the air

+ How you feel physically, emotionally, mentally, and spiritually

+ The vibrancy of the foliage around you. Are there trees, plants, and flowers nearby? What color are they? Do they have a fragrance? Are there birds, butterflies, dragonflies, or animals with you? What else is there?

When you have established this place in your mind, you will be able to return to it no matter where you are or what's going on around you. It will be there for you whenever you need it.

PRACTICE: WHAT MAKES YOU FEEL JOYFUL?

Think of this practice as an investigation into happiness, and let what you write inform you about your connection with joy. Then start to notice which experiences in your life make you really happy and which ones don't. Sometimes the best way to know what makes us happiest is figuring out what doesn't make us happy.

— TO DO THE PRACTICE —

Make a list of words that evoke a feeling of joy. Take the words you've jotted down and write a couple of sentences on each of them, describing what you experience most about the individual words.

1 What activity are you doing when you feel these emotions?

2 How do you feel in your body when you are doing this activity?

+ What is the quality of your breath?

+ Is your mind clear and focused?

+ Do you have a feeling of safety?

3 How could you bring more of this activity into your life and feel supported by the happiness it brings you?

These are some of mine:

Kindness	Compassion	Forgiveness
Generosity	Calmness	Positivity
Laughter	Reflection	Patience

Set your imagination free. Build on what makes you feel best when times are tough. You could transform a room to hold your treasures—photos of loved ones, flowers, and your meditation space—or it can be an activity like taking a walk on a favorite trail or taking your dog to the dog park to see familiar, friendly faces.

In my life I find security in cooking, cleaning, being in nature, and laying a hot water bottle on my chest after a challenging day. It matters less about what the activity is and more about how it makes you feel. This is a valuable tool, one that you can call on as a loyal friend to help lift your spirits in difficult times. It will encourage you to keep going when you want to throw your arms in the air and give up, and it will help you build an infrastructure for deep healing.

PRACTICE: VALIDATION

Without the simple step of recognizing our trauma, we replay the story, the sadness, and all of what it has taken from our lives over and over again. The importance of validation must not be underestimated. Validating the loss will support you in letting go of the story and allow you to take the next steps in healing. Give yourself permission to know the impact of your trauma on your life so you can get on with your life.

Note: If the circumstances of your life feel too frightening to revisit without the support of a therapist, do not move ahead with this practice.

— TO DO THE PRACTICE —

Find a place in your home or office where you can be alone and undisturbed. Make it a place where you feel very safe. Bring a journal, a pen, a timer, tissues, and anything else that helps you feel supported. Set your timer for three to six minutes. You may want to start with three minutes and work up to six minutes depending on how you feel going into the practice. As always, honor where you are before you start.

Trauma in your life may involve a variety of factors. For this practice I address the most pressing feelings in this moment. These emotions might be connected with what happened long ago or what may be happening right now in your life. It doesn't really matter what the details are. What are you feeling in this moment? Stand witness to your feelings without judgment, hear them, experience them, and validate them so you can release them.

Now write the first things that come to your mind when you ask these three questions.

1 What did this event take from your life?

2 What injustices did this event impose on your life?

3 What would your life be like had this not happened?

When you have completed your journaling for that day, take the sheets of paper and find a place where you can safely burn the contents, such as a fireplace or an outdoor fire pit. As you ceremonially light the paper, ask, "Do I need to revisit this again tomorrow?" If yes, make time to do this exercise again the next day. Ask this question every time you do this ritual until you feel the story let go of you.

After your burning ceremony is complete, take a comfortable seat and read the intention below or an intention of your own that you have created. Complete the ceremony with gratitude for the experience.

Intention

I have suffered the effects of:

_____

_____

_____

_____

(fill in the event that has brought you suffering). I have felt the sadness it has brought to my life. Thank you for bringing to light the parts of me that call for healing. I am grateful, and now I am ready to release the hurt and anger and move on.

THE INNER CHILD RETURNS HOME

Before I could nurture my inner child home again, I had to understand the survival traits I had taken on to make it through all that I had lost. I validated the abandonment in my own heart, recognized the devastation it created, and mourned what it took from me. The process was similar to that of losing a loved one, but now it was the most vulnerable parts of me I was mourning. There was no changing what had happened, so what I needed to do was figure out how to change the way I addressed the suffering.

I had adopted a defensive posturing to ward off hurt. I became guarded around any situation that made me feel tentative and vulnerable. After I would react in a certain way, I'd wonder why I had said those hurtful words or acted aggressively. These traits were old ways of being that no longer worked for me and were damaging those I loved. They were all based around fear, and they were bringing more fear into my life.

As this protective approach no longer supported the type of life I yearned for, I started to pay attention to my defensive behaviors. Once I became familiar with these worn-out survival traits, it became easier to notice when they showed up. I made up my mind to replace them with gentler, more loving practices. I nurtured the child in me with meditation, yoga, journaling, and other self-care practices that soothed and healed me. With this awareness, my emotions shifted rapidly. I started to feel more empowered and more confident that I was capable of transforming these disturbing survival techniques. I was no longer the child that had been left. I was a young woman with a desire to make my life better and to contribute to my family and community in loving and powerful ways. This consciousness softened me inside. This is how I started preparing a safe place inside for my inner child to return home.

AWARENESS OF OLD, WORN-OUT HABITS

The poem *"Please Hear What I'm Not Saying"* by Charles C. Finn helped me identify these survival traits. This is an excerpt from the poem.

Don't be fooled by me.
Don't be fooled by the face I wear
for I wear a mask, a thousand masks,
masks that I'm afraid to take off,
and none of them is me.

Pretending is an art that's second nature with me,
but don't be fooled,
for God's sake don't be fooled.
I give you the impression that I'm secure,
that all is sunny and unruffled with me, within as well as without,
that confidence is my name and coolness my game,
that the water's calm and I'm in command
and that I need no one,
but don't believe me.

My surface may seem smooth but my surface is my mask,
ever-varying and ever-concealing.
Beneath lies no complacence.
Beneath lies confusion, and fear, and aloneness.
But I hide this. I don't want anybody to know it.
I panic at the thought of my weakness exposed....

The poem is about trauma and the imprint it leaves on us when it is not resolved and healed. When I first read it, I felt like the universe had thrown me a lifeline. Through this poem, I saw my survival techniques in living color. I came to see that they were a double-edged sword. In many ways they saved my life. They protected me and allowed me to develop coping skills to carry on, but as I grew older, more capable, and independent, these behaviors no longer applied to my life. I knew that being burdened by low self-esteem, hypervigilance, anxiety around change, and fear of loss and abandonment were there, but what I didn't know before was how much they affected everything in my life. A life of keeping up appearances was exhausting me, and I acted out from that exhaustion.

When I read this poem, I felt like someone finally understood me. Dealing with trauma can be so very lonely, and often we can feel there is no way out of the destructive behaviors we are stuck in. But there is. I felt validated, pardoned for the many ways I had mistreated my life and hurt others in the process. Finally someone put words to what I was feeling. This poem helped me take the next steps to healing myself. With each healing step I learned more about how to take care of myself, how to love myself, and ultimately how to encourage my inner child back inside me. A little forward motion each day meant that someday I'd be free of the bondage of my hurt from the losses of my young life.

My continued healing would be dependent on awareness of my survival traits and the behaviors, habits, and reactions that triggered them. The more consciousness I brought to these habits, the less power they had over me. They were still there, as they would always be—I couldn't erase my personal history—but now they were just subtle reminders of needing to take extra care of myself.

My world was broken open by awareness. I was growing more in touch with who I was and how best to take care of my mind, body, heart, and spirit. I was making decisions that supported my healing, and each time I aligned myself with my heart and not my fearful mind, my world opened up to new possibilities.

HOW CHALLENGE MADE ME STRONGER

My story began with pain and loss but led me to a path that freed me from my suffering. It recovered the parts of me that had given up. As one of my beloved teachers says, "It is not despite the swamp that the lotus grows so beautifully, it is because of the swamp that it knows its magnificence." All the difficult stuff in my life encouraged me to find self-healing. It helped me learn how to nurture myself from the inside out and grow strong and courageous enough to begin again, time and time again. Adversity has made me stronger and has given me the tools I needed to heal and grow. I stopped running from people, places, and things that scared me and instead turned toward them. This is the miracle of my life.

I spent a long time feeling that I was not valuable enough in my parents' lives for them to stay, but I no longer believe that to be true. I have faith and forgiveness for my parents. I understand that they did the best they could with the circumstances of their lives. I look over my shoulder at my life and see all the healing gifts that have appeared to help me move forward. I feel blessed to have heard the messages of my body, the longings of my heart, and the awakenings of my spirit. Each of their messages gave me hope to continue on. I am no longer dependent on my outer environment to be perfect in order for me to know peace. I can find that peace anywhere, at any time, and in any situation. This is what I hope you will come to understand as you continue reading this book.

It is your time to know this power. There is no time to waste. Look in the mirror of your life and observe the powerful, courageous, frightened, faithful, forgiving human that looks back at you and says, "Put your seatbelt on, we're going for the ride of our lives, and it's going to be incredible!"

chapter 3

Trauma Comes in All Shapes and Forms

- -

Trauma is one of those words that frightens people. We tend to think of trauma as identifying a situation or circumstance that implies some sort of enormous tragedy, like a war incident, a rape, a murder, or some other situation that tears life apart. There is no doubt that these are traumas, but what we don't always give truth to is that trauma can come in all shapes and forms just like we do as humans. What affects you adversely may not be what affects me as powerfully, but that doesn't mean that it hasn't left you different than you were before it happened.

What does seem to be universal, though, is that trauma can be defined as an event that once experienced leaves an imprint on your life that affects everything you do moving forward. In other words, it didn't roll off your back as so many of our life experiences do. You will carry it around until you give it the time and energy it requires to move and heal through it. When there are unresolved issues resulting from trauma, minor events become major events very easily. Like the conversation with a friend that doesn't go the way you want it to go, or the traffic jam that held up your already tight schedule. The emotional effects of these events can wreak havoc on our system and in a state of trauma can snowball into overwhelming overreactions very easily.

Many of us who've suffered through trauma immediately deny that it exists in our lives. This may be because of a stigma or shame that is associated with an incident or a state of denial that removes you from feeling the effects of what an event brought to your life. I understand both of these relationships to trauma and many others, as I too avoided dealing with the events that brought trauma into my own life.

DISTINGUISHING BETWEEN HARD TRAUMA AND SOFT TRAUMA

There are two different forms of trauma. Hard trauma is recognized by having an identifiable beginning and end that is shocking and outside the norm of human experience. Violent death, natural disasters, personal assaults, and wartime tragedies are examples of hard trauma. These experiences immediately inform us that something life-changing has happened.

Soft trauma is not as easily identifiable or understood. It can show up as longtime abuse, the neglect of someone we depend on, or the unresolved presence of sorrow, anger, and resentment in our lives. It takes courage to reveal soft trauma and to step away from it because it often involves our family culture and the disruption of dysfunctional behaviors and habits within it. When there is one person who steps up and says that this way of being no longer works for her, everyone in that close-knit group is affected.

In this book and in my practice, my focus is on soft trauma. I have worked with many clients who are resistant to accepting that any type of trauma exists in their lives. They ask, "What would my life look like if I admitted it was there?" Change is very difficult, and when we change, we also alter the dynamics of how our families function. But without an awareness of the effects of soft trauma on our lives, we can never shift out of our wounded state.

Soft trauma includes:

* Abusive relationships, especially in childhood
  + absence of love, withheld affection
  + alcoholic or drug-abusing parent or partner
  + constant arguing in the home
  + physical or verbal abuse
  + pressure to keep family problems secret
  + pretense that internal disruption is normal
  + prolonged psychological abuse
* Diagnosis of major illness
* End of a relationship or marriage
* Financial hardship
* Grief
* Job loss or other professional disappointment
* Public humiliation

Surprisingly, soft trauma can be more difficult to heal through because it is harder to detect than the very apparent and extreme expressions of hard trauma. But each time you take a step in the direction of rediscovering your authentic life, you will feel the support of the universe come to you. And that will encourage you to keep going and help break down the walls that have kept you from your magnificent self.

IDENTIFYING TRAUMA IN YOUR LIFE

Many of us don't recognize that trauma exists in our lives; what we do know is that life hurts and we want it to feel different. There's a cloud that hangs over us that we can never quite shake. We get used to the discouraging situations and instead of investigating the root of the sadness, we find ways to live with it.

Our systems—physical, emotional, mental, and spiritual—are highly sensitive and incredibly powerful. When we recognize trauma and take steps to heal through it, miracles happen that we never imagined possible.

An important first step is to identify the trauma causing you pain. The following are some of the symptoms of hidden trauma.

Physical symptoms of trauma

* Autoimmune conditions
* Chronic pain
* Digestive issues
* Eating disorders
* Unexpected or difficult-to-explain sickness

Emotional symptoms of trauma

* Overwhelming sadness or numbness
* Anxiety
* Depression
* Low self-esteem
* Post-traumatic stress flashbacks
* Relationship challenges
* Oversensitivity

Mental symptoms of trauma

* Addictions
* Persistent fear
* Compulsive behaviors
* Financial struggles
* Panic attacks
* Hypervigilance

Spiritual symptoms of trauma

* Loss of connection to nature and things you love
* Estrangement from self and community
* Inability to tap into anything that brings happiness
* Inability to envision a bright future

As you look over this list, you might think, "How can all of these count as traumas? They're just *normal life*." You would be right: death, disappointment, and fear enter into everyone's life at some point or other. That means that *everyone* has some firsthand experience with trauma—but not everyone processes trauma the same way. Some people have the resources, personal strength, and support system to heal through it right away, while others in a weakened state have no ability to process the disruption and devastation. What does trauma look like when it lingers unresolved?

A common symptom of trauma is that these negative feelings and actions don't come and go; they show up and stay with us, whether as a low hum in the background of our lives or a loud bang that won't let us go. If we anesthetize these feelings with destructive coping skills, we will be affected by them for the rest of our lives.

Common destructive coping skills include:

* Throwing yourself into relationships
* Overworking
* Compulsive behaviors
* Bingeing on alcohol, drugs, food, sex, TV/video games, and or shopping

As human beings we are biologically designed to survive all sorts of disruption. If that were not the case, we would be extinct. Disturbing events exist in our lives in one form or another. Depending on how we interact with the disturbances, we will either carry forward an emotional imprint from the event or not. If we have been impacted negatively, we will need to release the experience. If left unattended, the emotions will mark and wound us. It is similar to what we experience physically when the body is compromised. If left unattended, there is potential for a more serious situation to arise. But if it is supported through awareness and encouraged to heal, there is a much better chance for full recovery.

PRACTICE: UNWINDING YOUR BODY

Here's an easy way of judging if you need to unwind: Stand tall, balancing equally on both feet. Close your eyes and notice how your body moves. If you feel yourself moving in small circles or side to side, your body would benefit from this release. This simple, playful exercise shows you how different it is to move from your spirit instead of your mind, and it has wonderful benefits for the overall system.

— TO DO THE PRACTICE —

1 Find a room with a clean area where you can be on the floor and roll around.

2 Imagine your energy has gotten all bound up, like a chord or a rope that needs unraveling.

3 Set an intention, such as: *I am going to unwind and release the bound-up energy in my body.*

4 Allow yourself to roll around in a way that is instructed by your spirit rather than your mind, and let go. It may feel a bit contorted at times, but do your best to go with it (always staying safe in the process).

5 When you have had enough, simply say, *I am done unwinding.* Lie down for a few minutes and allow the experience to sink in and heal you at a very deep level.

SEEKING HELP IN THE WRONG PLACES

So often we choose not to look at pain because it feels too overwhelming. We have already lived through the trauma once; why on earth would we go back and do it again? The ego says *no way.* We do our best to avoid revisiting any part of what hurt us, but this kind of avoidance isn't supportive of long-term healing. The imprint from the trauma has been set, and there are only two directions we can move in, toward the disturbance or away from it. Sadly, most of our society moves away from it and goes to outrageous lengths to not feel the pain again.

Sometimes in an effort to deflect the pain of trauma we can dump our fearful emotions on others in an effort to release toxic emotions. This is a dangerous practice. Not only does it have the potential to hurt those we love, but it can further cycle our own suffering, never allowing us to get to the source of the pain. Most times you don't get the reaction and support you need because your friend, family member, or significant other doesn't have the training needed to assist you in healing and moving through the trauma. It may sound familiar: the loved one wants to help but doesn't have the objectivity needed to do so, and soon it becomes too personal and overwhelming; you feel ashamed for opening up and grow frustrated, and soon you're worse off than you were before you engaged them.

Pay close attention to what you ask from those closest to you. The treasured relationships that we have with family and friends should be honored and they shouldn't be burdened with requests that they are not qualified to help us with. When you make the decision to heal, give yourself every chance to do so. Seeking professional help including a trained therapist and health care provider is one of the most important steps you can take. Find a therapist who is trained in trauma and who can guide you to other professionals who can further support you. These might include a massage therapist, chiropractor, acupuncturist, holistic medical doctor, naturopath, yoga teacher, meditation teacher, Reiki practitioner, and/or Ayurvedic healer. We will go into this more in Chapter 4.

GETTING STUCK IN THE SURVIVAL MIND-SET

Humans are complex creatures, and it constantly amazes me how we can grow in some ways and remain stuck in other ways. When I started to face my trauma, I was a nonstop, multitasking businesswoman, wife, and mom—and yet I still approached emotional problems with the logic of a heartbroken thirteen-year-old. The trauma I faced in my teens caused me to stop developing emotionally and spiritually. I was in survival mode even years after the danger had passed.

Many people are stuck in a similar emergency mind-set. These are the people who never seem to have a quiet, happy month, or week, or day in some cases. Every moment of discomfort or uncertainty—even a small inconvenience—in their lives is treated as a disaster. (And when there is a *real* disaster, watch out, it gets intense.) They can't get out of their own way, and personal growth and professional success become very difficult for them to achieve. Calmness or thoughtfulness are out of reach; all of their energy goes into surviving the assaults of their day-to day-existence.

In a balanced life, an inconvenience or moment of tension is naturally processed and released without our knowing. When the coping mechanisms aren't operating correctly, trifling moments of discomfort can overwhelm us tremendously. Those of us living with existing states of trauma need to be self-aware and watch feelings that arise in these situations.

CYCLING THROUGH TRAUMA AGAIN AND AGAIN

When trauma happens in childhood, it can be difficult to understand how it has affected you, because you basically have been in a state of trauma for your *entire life*. So much of what you did then to compensate for the pain has become part of your everyday routine. You carry on with your life, making adjustments as needed, not realizing that your coping mechanisms have been overloaded.

One of the biggest clues that unresolved trauma is affecting your life is looking at what you are attracting in your life. It could be relationships that fail in a similar way each time or the inability to hold a job because the same "annoying people" show up wherever you are. Or maybe it's that you constantly feel taken advantage of by family and friends and don't understand why your nearest and dearest don't pay you more respect. When we don't fully release trauma, there is often an impulse to cycle through the specific trauma again and again, recreating the circumstances with someone new each time until we figure it out. It becomes a painful loop of events.

Dysfunction and disorder show up for a reason. They are a message from deep within, beckoning you toward healing. I know how uncomfortable this may feel, but every tiny step in the direction of healing your heart is an opportunity to gain strength and contentment. For me, there was no alternative. The lifestyle of blame, shame, and self-loathing was taking me down. I knew I needed to feel empowered by my life, not trod upon. In this way trauma became a partner of mine. It helped me recognize and feel my suffering and motivated me to heal through it. The tremendously hopeful news is that once you have acknowledged that trauma has occurred in your life, every healing opportunity is available to you.

PRACTICE: FINDING YOUR RELATIONSHIP TO TRAUMA

It is very hard to revisit events that have caused us pain. But when we find the strength to go back and really feel the impact of our experience, we have more of a chance of resolving the inner pain and the disturbances that pain creates in our lives when unresolved.

— TO DO THE PRACTICE —

Find a quiet place that feels safe, then ask yourself the questions on page 48. But before you set out, understand that what appears could bring up difficult emotions like judgment, shame, or embarrassment. If so, relate to these emotions as words only and avoid feeding into a storyline that takes your attention from the practice before you. Open your heart to whatever shows up. When you turn the mirror toward yourself, you have all the power needed to change anything and everything in your life. This is your chance to reset old habits and pave the way for new, revitalizing ways of being to take form.

Be sure to write down your questions and answers in your journal so you can reread them and feel how they resonate in your body, mind, and spirit. This is just the beginning of understanding what you feel inside, and these questions are just some examples of what to ask. Feel free to build on these questions, get as creative as you like, and tailor your line of questioning to the events specific to your life.

1 Are you easily overwhelmed?

2 Does stress overwhelm you?

3 Do you load one enormous event on top of another?

4 Do you take your time to assess the situation in front of you before you act out?

5 Do you make good decisions under pressure?

6 Do you regret your actions or second-guess yourself often?

DISCONNECTING FROM THE BODY, MIND, AND SPIRIT WHEN TRAUMA HITS

It is not unusual to leave the body, mind, and spirit when trauma hits. After all, who wants to be present for the extreme hurt that a painful event brings up? Understanding that this is a normal default is a great start because it brings awareness to how we react when uncomfortable situations occur. But it is vital to our healing process that we feel the effects of the trauma in our whole being, so we can validate the hurt and let it go. Otherwise we aren't able to understand the message the hurt brings us and we continually push it away.

To demonstrate the importance of being connected to the body, even in moments of pain, we can take a lesson from nineteenth-century midwifery. Without the pain medications we have today, mothers-to-be would manage their labor pains by energetically leaving their bodies. But the midwife would need the mother present in body, mind, and spirit to support the birth, so they used herbs, in particular rosemary, to coax them back to the present moment to ensure a successful delivery. The natural tendencies of our body, mind, and spirit to protect us by removing us from the present moment when life gets too painful are an instinctual mechanism to take care of us. But just as valuable as this instinctual mechanism is the awareness that this disconnection has happened. It is from that place of awareness and connection to our consciousness that we have the chance to move forward.

DISCOVERING
A NEW WAY OF BEING AFTER ANXIETY

Dealing with anxiety and panic attacks was a normal way of being for me. The highs and lows of anxiety were a part of my life, even something I had become dependent upon to make me feel alive. This is often what happens with anxiety: you weave panic into your life because you know no other way of being; it is your reality, so you make the most of it, accepting the frantic state as who you are. The real mind-blower comes when you have an experience of yourself that offers you a glimmer of what life could feel like *without* the extreme anxiety fluctuations, without the drama.

When we have a sense of how life can be without extreme ups and downs, room opens up in our lives. We've made space to release the burden of anxiety. We have a different experience altogether now. Life no longer demands the highly regulated attention of an anxious way of being.

I felt great success when at last I could notice when anxiety came in, recognize its trigger, and then let it go. My anxiety no longer had the upper hand. I knew it was there when it showed up, but I knew how to handle it. I no longer needed to run from it, because it didn't scare me anymore.

LEARNING THAT IT'S NEVER TOO LATE TO HEAL

A beloved client of mine lost his ten-year-old son as a result of a doctor's mistake. His son had been given a drug for a minor infection, which initially "cured" it, until the infection aggressively returned. The family could hardly bear this loss. The injustice felt too great to overcome. They were a large family with five other children. My client, the father of the child, coped by burying himself in his work, which he did—for the next forty years. At retirement, life and busyness slowed down and the unresolved trauma crept back in. He had no more energy to fight away the sadness. He needed to find peace from an event he'd been running from his whole adult life.

In our time together we spoke a lot about the emotions that surrounded the loss. He explained how he felt helpless and responsible for the doctor's mistake and how he had really never forgiven himself for what happened. After he verbalized his emotions, I guided him through some breathing exercises that allowed him to process the words he had never been able to say out loud. He experienced the mind-body-spirit connection for the first time that afternoon. He was astounded at how he had lost touch with himself through the trauma. Now what he really wanted most was to find his way to the peace and calm of a compassionate life.

Months later he came back to tell me how his personal practice had guided him to work in a hospice house and how the experience was offering him the chance to help others find peace in the last stages of their lives too. He was teaching these people to recognize their loss and find calm as they took their last breaths.

I often see people give up, fearful that there is no time left to find peace, but this magnificent example of bravery shows us how it is never too late to do the healing work of your life.

FINDING FORGIVENESS

Unkind acts can cut very deep, and moving beyond them can be our life's work. It is easy to understand how we can get stuck in what has happened and create storylines around traumatic events for a long time, reliving the devastation or even perpetuating the pain in new relationships and life decisions. I have found that some of this recycling is necessary. It is important that we process what has happened to us and how it has hurt us. But at a certain point the process no longer helps us heal. It becomes a heavy weight of remembrance that is imbedded in our nervous system and affects everything we do. Forgiveness is one of the most effective ways of breaking the cycle to begin the process of healing at all levels. The forgiveness journey transforms you. When we hold on to anger, it resonates in our being. For some people it may be a very subtle undertone of feeling and for others far more apparent, but any amount of unresolved hurt eventually will affect you and those around you.

If this concept doesn't resonate with you at this moment, don't worry. The act of asking the question "How much anger and resentment live in me in this moment?" is a powerful exercise in awareness in itself and a perfect place to start. Be honest with yourself; evaluate where you are truthfully, and move ahead. There will be plenty of other opportunities to look at forgiveness. As you grow stronger, feelings of compassion and ultimately forgiveness will show up; just watch. For now, hold steady to your commitment to self-care and trust that the rest will come.

HEALING THROUGH TRAUMA IS A HEROIC ACT

One of my favorite authors and greatest teachers, Joseph Campbell, describes the process of healing through trauma as a hero's journey. In the famous documentary *Bill Moyers and the Power of Myth,* Campbell says that the hero is "a person that has found a supernormal range of human and spiritual life and then comes back to communicate it…It's a cycle." The cycle he speaks of is the birth and death of the inner fears that keep us from all we hope to achieve in this lifetime. The quest that allows us to defeat the fear is in fact the biggest achievement of our life: it is a heroic act. When we find the strength to slay the inner dragon of the mind and ego through self-love, we have the opportunity to become the hero in our lives.

Directly revisiting an experience that has brought so much pain takes strength, vision, determination, and a belief in hope for something better. When something traumatic happens, most people's first reaction is to shut down in fear. We've all seen this happen in our own lives and on television at a crime scene with witnesses screaming, blaming, and emotionally breaking down. Then, every once in a while, the hero appears, the person who acts courageously and has the wherewithal to contribute in a seemingly superhuman way. Their courage can tap into a deeper part of us and ignite hope in an otherwise terrifying situation.

Observing the hero in someone else helps us feel and recognize our own inner hero. As our consciousness lifts, we heal, grow, and live life in a happier way. Joseph Campbell's message tells us to keep up, persevere, and find ways of strengthening ourselves on this hero's path.

Ultimately, you are the only one who can slay your dragons of fear and lack of love for yourself. It's up to you to conquer the challenges that keep you from your greatest joys. There will be mentors, teachers, and guides who will show up to revitalize you on your path, but they will not be able to do the work for you. Only you can be the hero in your own story.

chapter 4

Putting a Plan for Self-Healing in Place

The creative spirit knows no boundaries. It is expansive, infinite, and ranges out there beyond the restrictive walls of mind and thought. It is transcendent, and our heroic life's quest is to find the strength to move toward those infinite boundaries. When we listen and connect to the spirit's calling, few questions are asked. It would be like asking the heart why it beats.

In this chapter I will help you to lay out a plan for an energetically fortified life—not in broad strokes, but in the moments of your life when everything happens. The mission is to learn, by heart, the tools you will need to stay afloat in the greatest tides of life. In a new place of self-awareness and self-love, you can listen to the call of your creative spirit and move toward a whole, happy, and peaceful way of being. Become a trailblazer who listens deeply, not to the noise of your surroundings but to the ever-present instructions of your spirit and the universe.

PREPARING THE WAY FOR SELF-HEALING

In life there are many opportunities to commit ourselves to someone else's system. We can slide into a plan without really thinking about it, going along with a dogma that isn't ours and obeying it for the rest of our lives. But what if that system doesn't work for us? What if it does more harm than good? If you're lucky, your strong, creative spirit will yearn to find its own way. What does it take to hear and heed your personal mission?

Committing to self-healing guides your energy to the road less traveled and reveals the path that's right for you. You'll go by road signs that say "Stop here, it's too dangerous ahead," but you are now equipped with the skills to move past obstacles that in the past would have stopped you in your tracks. Now you choose methods for healing rather than coping skills that numb you from the experience.

At this point in the book, I hope you are beginning to feel the deeper aspects of who you are. Your practices are guiding you inside. Yes, these inquiries may be stirring up all sorts of emotions, but you are building an architecture to support those emotions. In strength you can hold what you could not hold before. Your experiences of self are encouraging you forward, even in the darkest nights of the soul. You are starting to understand that the lessons of life are no longer daunting and insurmountable. Hardship has a purpose; the only thing you have to do is find enough personal power to embrace it and learn from its lessons.

The key to staying on the path is knowing your truth, having an awareness of where you are, and sticking with a self-discipline that holds you steady on the path of healing. Being aware of your energy means that you replenish your strength before you've even noticed that you are starting to grow weak. Self-care is easiest when you have a structure in place to sustain it. Teachers and teachings can guide, but they are only effective with a good foundation in place.

In the past I was drawn to teachings that I thought would change my life but didn't because I wasn't strong enough to sustain the practice. I would start to feel like I had finally found a teacher who could guide me away from my confusing cycle of suffering, but I would end up quitting in despair. The work was too hard for me at that point, and my low self-esteem and discouraged spirit couldn't keep up. The only way to break through the suffering of the mind was to go deeper into the pain and find the teacher within.

FINDING THE TEACHER WITHIN

Sometimes we are good at guiding ourselves toward happiness, and sometimes we falter. In order for us to learn from anyone else, we have to learn to be guided by our own compass first. When we don't have strength, courage, security, and confidence, aligning ourselves with our inner compass can feel unobtainable. Knowing how much you trust your own instincts could be the best information that you gather about yourself. Understand where you are on your own path. Be truthful with your expectations and progress. When you meet yourself with honesty, everything is possible. Embrace yourself in understanding and compassion and set a course for your life that guides you back to your true north, back to yourself.

It is tempting to hope that someone out there will do this work for you and help you figure out how to take care of yourself, but no one can do it for you. No one other than you can heal your body, mind, heart, and spirit. My work is not about helping you find another lesson or teacher outside of yourself. It's about nurturing you back home to that place inside you where your weary heart can deeply rest and your spirit can wake up, trust, and go beyond the limited mind. When you connect to your life from an internal center of peace, everything is possible. The hard work of life is released, because now you know that even the most difficult situations of life have a purpose. Every step you take toward fulfilling your purpose, even the tiniest of steps, reinforces your faith in yourself and in your connection to the transcendent forces alive in your life.

Through my healing journey, one of the most profound concepts I have embraced is personal accountability. I have the opportunity to make whatever magic I want to create in my life with my practice. The only things holding me back from my fabulous life are my own restrictive ways of being and bad habits that have me thinking and acting negatively. There is no greater gift than waking up to myself and taking responsibility for how I interact with the world. I am my own first teacher.

BECOMING A DEVOTED LISTENER

There are so many reasons we avoid listening to our life's messages. After all, those messages aren't always kind to us. We typically look outside of ourselves to help us interpret disruptions in our lives. In times of stress and upheaval, our perspective gets tainted by our insecurities, especially if we haven't yet learned how to believe in ourselves.

When you are filled with negativity and self-doubt, it's possible that you might reach inside and receive a message from your body or about your body that is cruel. I understand this with all my heart. I suspect it is the very reason that many of us push the idea of meditation away. When people talk about their inability to meditate, in other words to sit alone, quietly, for minutes at a time, I hear them say, "I can't sit still that long. My mind won't stop. My body hurts. I get agitated when I am still. I have too much else to do." These honest answers express a warning of deeper tension inside. That resistance likely means that there is something uncomfortable ahead and you should not open the dialogue lightly.

The time will come to face your fears and that which you've been avoiding. Whatever words, feelings, or images fill the silence when you turn inward, they have been waiting a long time to be heard, felt, and seen. It might sting, but then there will be relief. You will have faced your demons, and you will be ready to move on toward gentle healing. Best of all, each time you make the effort to direct your focus inward, you will become a better listener. You won't have to wait until your feelings are screaming at you to be heard. With a daily practice, you will routinely give your feelings a chance to be listened to, felt, and figured out, and with that in place, you will begin the extremely potent practice of healing. You can liken the practice of listening to cleaning up an overgrown garden. At one time, the garden flourished, but for lack of paying attention the weeds have taken over, and now it needs great care. The gardener holds a memory of what the garden was like in all its beauty and balance, and instead of turning away from it now, something has inspired her to walk toward it and dig into the soil again. Few questions are asked, for something deep inside her has called her back. That instinct is all she knows right now. The pull is strong, and she listens. She knows it's a big decision, but she also knows that the benefits will be bountiful. For under those weeds, brambles, and vines still exists a beautiful garden that can be brought back to life with the proper nourishment. But what calls her back most is the way the garden makes her feel when she is near it. The garden wakes up a part of her that is asleep when she is away from its beauty, and this turning away has become too much for her to bear. So instead she heads over to her garden, and with every step she takes, the path becomes clearer and clearer.

This is the very way we prune back the weeds and insecurities of our lives. We listen to the messages of the body, mind, heart, and spirit and learn what we need to do to restore and revitalize our lives. This beauty exists in us now. It has just become overgrown with old experiences and outgrown feelings that choke our view. There will be hard work. Yes, it will reveal pain, hurt, and discomfort, but for a good reason. This time the pain will be felt *and healed*. This time you go in ready to excavate your beauty; you know it's there, and you are prepared to do anything needed to restore it. You have become a devoted listener.

CREATING A PLACE OF REST INSIDE YOURSELF

All paths lead home when we prioritize the love of self first. You have come this far. The hardest work is done, because you have decided to look deeper than the symptoms of your life. There is a conviction in your actions that was not there before. You are learning how to care for yourself deeply, and with this knowledge, everything is possible.

The ability to know what feels right for you is your starting point. You will burn out vital personal resources if you do not have a clear gauge as to what makes you happy, when it is time to give out to others, and when it is time to come back home to rest. This is the time when life becomes less complicated, less confusing, and easier all around. Nothing is left up to guesswork; the trail is marked clearly, because you have a true sense of what it takes to make you feel safe and happy in the many situations of your life.

For those of us who have lived in pain, reconnecting to that peaceful place inside becomes the mission of our lives. When we have faith and are open to healing at this deep level, miraculous shifts of consciousness happen. When we build a relationship with safety and security and have established a place for our hearts to rest, we are not afraid to experience life's disruptions. We observe how challenges can help us grow and learn. We no longer feel the need to run from fearful triggers. Instead we can see what they bring up in us, meet their inquiry, and build strength from this place of knowledge.

Remember that when feelings of discouragement, frustration, and rage come up, there are signposts within them guiding us to the next successes. Be willing to learn what you have to do to make yourself feel safe, and do it. That way you can take a brave look at your life and begin the beautiful, courageous process of recovering from the trauma in your life.

PRACTICE: FINDING A SAFE PLACE WITHIN

1 Imagine a place anywhere in the world that represents safety to you. Make it a place in your mind that feels tremendously safe. In your mind's eye, build it out in a way that you are able to see, feel, and hear it. See the light. Listen to the sounds. Take in the smells. Notice how your environment feels on your skin. Use your breath to get there. Feel the comfort that this place invokes in you.

2 Spend time in your safe place and know that you can access its safety at any time and from anywhere. This is the place you'll rest your heart.

3 Let your creative mind have free reign. Then go to this place anytime you feel unsafe, be it on a physical, emotional, mental, or spiritual level.

4 Do this practice as often as you can today, and keep building on it throughout the week.

YOUR HEALING JOURNEY HAS NO TIMETABLE

Healing doesn't work with a measured type of progress. This is an adventure that you will be on for the rest of your life. Once you have that understanding, you can let go of the pressure to succeed and stay open to what appears going forward in your life. You are gathering the provisions you need to make that journey inward. Each step you take in that direction will enable you to look at your greatest dreams and move toward them. The only thing separating any of us from our greatest dreams is our fear. Take the pressure off and start to have fun. Be curious, open, and forgiving of yourself as you learn, and know that in that place everything is possible.

The only thing that keeps me from making progress is disconnecting myself from my joy of living. When I become resentful, angry, and blaming of others, my life's energy is cut off from me. When I get separated from my bliss by the unexpected hardships of life, I know it. Everything feels heavy: my body hurts, my mind feels trapped and overwhelmed, and I often look for escape routes in unhelpful places. The difference now is that I can catch myself when this starts to happen and stop it before it gets worse. I can look at my needs and heal myself. When I move forward, each time I'm a little bit stronger. It is easy to say and harder to do, and sometimes we can get off course. But when we do, we know how to reconnect with our source of joy and guide ourselves back to safety.

RECONNECTING WHEN LIFE
TAKES YOU OFF COURSE

I've learned many important lessons when I have lost my way on my path of healing. During these times I would get discouraged and feel like I was failing, until I realized that this was just the nature of learning. To understand that I had lost my way meant that I was paying attention to my life, enough to know when I was lost. I could see the difference between where I had been, where I was, and where I wanted to be. This might sound funny, but honestly, many people lose their way and never realize they are lost, and instead they carry on in pain and confusion and are out of sync with their true nature.

Notice carefully when you are in harmony with your true nature. Experience what it feels like to be there and what it feels like to be separated from that place. Start to look at your life in its entirety—the physical, emotional, mental, and spiritual—with the understanding that none of these entities exists without the others. Notice if one of them screams louder than the others, and be willing to ask what you can do to heal it. If you are willing to listen closely, information will come through. This kind of practice takes time to trust, but it will serve you well if you can keep at it. Because we haven't been taught to travel inward, it can feel awkward and silly at first, but when you trust what comes through, it's hard to deny the potency of this source of energy in your life.

TUNING INTO OUR
ENERGY THROUGH THE CHAKRAS

The energy of life is something we all have a relationship with, whether we pay attention to it or not. How do you gauge whether you feel strong or tired? You measure your energy level. How do you express enthusiasm for something? With an energetic response. How do you describe someone's personality? By the energy they radiate. As a student and athlete, I certainly had a relationship with energy in this way—but it wasn't until later that I realized I could support and distribute my energy in a way that would make a real difference in my life. I did this by learning about the chakras.

The chakras are energy points in our subtle body (rather than the physical body) where our life force moves. The word *chakra* in Sanskrit translates to "wheel," and these wheels of energy—there are eight main ones—relate to who we are on a physical and spiritual level. The chakras connect with each other and move throughout the body, beginning with the first chakra at the base of the spine up to the eighth chakra above the head. They start with the most primal needs of the body, working upward like a ladder that reaches toward our full spiritual potential. The basic theory underlying the chakra system is that every human body has a certain amount of energy that is as real and important as any other bodily system and must be respected and taken care of for us to realize true health.

Before I was introduced to the chakra system, I knew that there were activities that made me feel alive, vibrant, and excited, and still other experiences, sensations, and circumstances that drained me. These experiences made me feel guilty and brought on huge amounts of resistance. But when I learned about the energetic anatomy and the specifics of the chakra system, it opened me to knowledge about myself that I had never before accessed. I had a whole new approach to how to take care of myself. I became in tune with my life as whole. I came to understand that my emotions and physical experiences were actually very much connected. This understanding helped me make sense of parts of my life that for so long had felt disconnected and disjointed. Now I understood what made my life work most efficiently. I could feel the impact of my mind, body, heart, and spirit and their dependence on one another. Then I took it one big step further and realized that *everything* in our life is connected.

The chakra information gave my life a blueprint that had not existed before. When I began to apply the principles of the chakra system to my healing rituals, meditation, yoga, and the food I ate, there was an overall nourishment in my life that I had not known before. The gift that this energetic chart offered me was that now I could see where I felt imbalances in my life and how they were affecting me. I understood now how the trauma of my young life had depleted certain energy centers more than others, like how the low back pain I suffered at a young age was connected with these losses and how my shortness of breath was related to my broken heart. This gave me a map for healing; as soon as

I started paying attention to my life from this new perspective, chronic issues started to heal. I was able to restore vitality to these energy centers through my self-care practices, yoga, meditation, and relationship with nature.

I am offering you the chakra chart here so you can integrate this knowledge visually. The chart illustrates the eight energy centers and where they reside. If this looks completely foreign to you, don't worry— it is merely a place to spark your interest. It is not important for you to become an expert on the chakras or to learn anything more than the interdependence of the energy centers. If it intrigues you, you can return and study it further at any point.

Notice on the chart how the first three chakras are the most primal, representing home, safety, security, procreation, and personal power. The first three chakras must be balanced before we can do any monumental healing (but as we know, what we address in one area of our life affects all the other aspects). Think of these centers as the base of your human structure and just like anything that flourishes, the foundation has to be strong to thrive. After the losses of my life, my greatest imbalances were found in the first three chakras. My energetic foundation was fragile. Safety and security had been shattered in my life, and I had very little trust in turning things around. I started to look at ways to create strength in my base. I reevaluated my primary relationships, home, career, and what made me most happy and what did not. At this time, I rediscovered my innocence. I started to see glimpses of my inner child, the part of me that believed life could feel safe and secure again, and most important, I started to feel deserving of this stability. As I strengthened my energy from the base up, I started to feel safety and happiness return to my life.

THE CHAKRA ENERGY SYSTEM

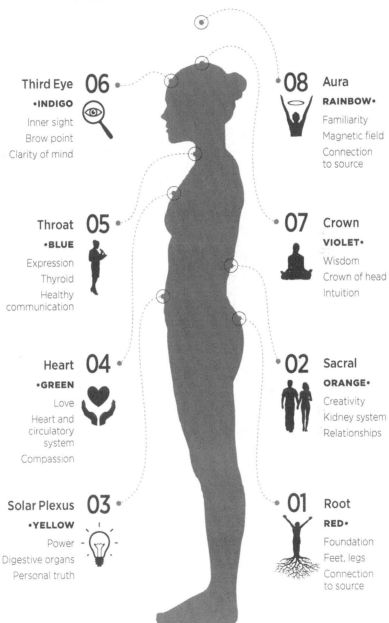

Third Eye 06
•INDIGO
Inner sight
Brow point
Clarity of mind

08 Aura
RAINBOW•
Familiarity
Magnetic field
Connection
to source

Throat 05
•BLUE
Expression
Thyroid
Healthy
communication

07 Crown
VIOLET•
Wisdom
Crown of head
Intuition

Heart 04
•GREEN
Love
Heart and
circulatory
system
Compassion

02 Sacral
ORANGE•
Creativity
Kidney system
Relationships

Solar Plexus 03
•YELLOW
Power
Digestive organs
Personal truth

01 Root
RED•
Foundation
Feet, legs
Connection
to source

Ideally we are taken care of by our loved ones until we learn the skills to take care of ourselves. But when events interrupt that natural nurturing process, the inner child is left unattended and imbalances occur. When I started to nurture what was most vulnerable, I learned that I could be the mother and the father of myself, and that's how I was able to reconnect with my inner child.

PRACTICE:
LAYING YOUR ENERGETIC FOUNDATION

This practice is designed to strengthen your energetic foundation to help you accept the ever-changing events of life.

1 Memorize the colors of each chakra, the word or short phrase that summarizes its meaning, and the body part where it resides:

+ **1st chakra:** red
  foundation, feet, legs, connection to source

+ **2nd chakra:** orange
  creativity, kidney sytem, relationships

+ **3rd chakra:** yellow
  power, digestive organs, personal truth

+ **4th chakra:** green
  love, heart and circulatory system, compassion

+ **5th chakra:** blue
  expression, thyroid, healthy communication

+ **6th chakra:** indigo
  inner sight, brow point, clarity of mind

+ **7th chakra:** violet
  wisdom, crown of head, intuition

+ **8th chakra:** rainbow colors or white
  magnetic field, connection to source

2 Write your chakra list down and keep it near your meditation space. Start your practice by placing your hands on your belly and taking a few long, deep breaths.

3 Say out loud: "First chakra." Breathe in deeply, focusing your attention on the chakra's body part, in this case your feet. Exhale. Breathe in again, picturing the color red. Welcome whatever shade or whatever red image appears to you. Breathe out and say: "Home." Breathe in again and welcome any images or feelings that appear. Continue speaking, breathing, and visualizing the remaining chakras in order.

4 When you are finished, close your eyes and envision all the colors together, like a rainbow. Don't worry if you can't line them up in order—just enjoy the rainbow in whatever form it shows up in your mind's eye.

BUILDING A FOUNDATION STRONG ENOUGH TO HANDLE CHANGE

Nature's law states that everything is forever changing. You can't stop the world from shifting, but you *can* change how you handle it. Life becomes a much gentler, richer journey when we become strong enough to accept and grow from what shows up. Think for a moment about how you deal with unexpected events: do they throw your world into a tailspin, or do you have the ability and stability to deal with them as they come up? Do you find yourself moving with the tides of your life or being resistant to them? Can you accept the raw feelings that surface when change feels unfair? Can you meet your experiences with unconditional acceptance or do you turn away from them and suffer? Whatever your answers, just notice them and use the information to grow from it. When we have a fragile energetic foundation, we aren't strong enough to look at fear and sadness. When we build a strong foundation, we give life permission to move through us freely without the barriers that fear brings on. In acceptance of the law of nature, amazing opportunities open to us and life becomes an adventure of one possibility to the next.

In learning how to develop a relationship to my energy system, I began to understand what it was that terrified me most—loss, sickness, emotional sadness, and even the smallest inconvenience or change in my routine. It was not like these obstacles were going to go away; they are a natural part of life. What I had to learn was how to love change. This was the challenge of my life. I had to embrace the beauty that change brought on: revitalization, space to grow, refreshed perspective, new friends, chances for success. I had to go with the flow instead of holding on tight to something that could never be stopped. I needed to build a foundation of healthy coping skills to deal with change.

Life by its very nature insists that we dance with the events that are in front of us. Dancing is a beautiful demonstration of transition, as its success demands cooperation. We've seen dancing partners who have accomplished this; they move in response to their partner's spontaneous cues by staying open to what comes up in the dance. The most talented partners look like they are one, not two separate people doing the dance. We can dance with life in partnership, accepting change as we meet it and bring strength, flexibility, and ultimately happiness to the process, or we can resist change and stand alone in our suffering.

There is a birth and death to life that happens continually, and until we find a way to accept this reality, life will feel tenuous. The world around is constantly changing. We have a gloomy day and then a spectacular one. The winter gives way to spring, which blooms into summer, and so on. The tides come in and out, as do the cycles of the moon. We watch our parents age and our children grow and yet still somehow we deny that time passes, clearing out the old and making way for the new. We fiercely hold on to what is in front of us instead of allowing time to pass like sand through our open hands. It is this type of grasping that restricts the flow of life, whereas acceptance gives way to the miracles of transition.

We know that we are not here on earth permanently, yet many of us deny this fact until the end of our life when we are too old to do what it takes to find grace in the greatest transition of life, death. Studies indicate that death is the number one fear in our lives. The biggest transition we face as humans is the reality that we are not here forever. Our loved ones will die, and so will we. My greatest fears were around loss, particularly the unprocessed death of my father when I was sixteen years old. Because of the circumstances surrounding my father's death, I did not grieve his loss until I was thirty. I compartmentalized the sadness and stuffed it away. These survival techniques worked for a while, then stopped working completely. Because I had unconciously compartmentalized this sadness for so long, when it appeared again it was unrecognizable to me and I didn't know what was causing my anxiety. I experienced panic attacks around the safety of my family and loved ones and had a hypervigilance toward life that was exhausting. This suffering was my trajectory for healing. I could no longer hide the grief of my father's death; the emotions were coming up to be healed, and I had no choice but to listen.

As humans, it is our tendency to want to hold on to happy, easier times, but it is this grasping and control that initiates discomfort and stops the flow of life. Life is made up alternately of pleasure and pain. Just as the hard times come, so do the good times. Like the tides of the ocean, one cannot exist without the other. There would be no crest to the wave without the undercurrent that supplies the force. The ocean would be flat and motionless and all would cease to thrive. Life will happen and there will be trauma, sadness, and grief; it is the very nature of life. It is also absolutely necessary to meet fear honestly by turning toward it instead of moving away from it.

Once again, there is no way to stop what life delivers during your time here on earth. It is nature's way of continually rejuvenating and regenerating the experiences of our human nature and higher nature. This is the magnificent gift of life, so why have we turned it into something that we fear and resent? There is a much bigger conversation to have on that question, but for now let's concentrate on self-love and the architecture we need to have in place to live at peace with the change.

CONQUERING INSTANT GRATIFICATION

I first learned about instant gratification when I read *The Road Less Traveled* by M. Scott Peck. Instant gratification is the quick fix. It is the go to—drugs, drink, sex, food, work—that distracts us from that which triggers pain in us.

In my young life, I had never looked at my own inability to move through pain. Avoidance of pain seemed like what I needed to do to take care of myself. To want to move away from discomfort is a natural survival instinct, but a valuable distinction is knowing when discomfort and pain are life-threatening and when they show up to help us heal. Pain is important for us to feel and experience so we can resolve and ultimately heal the issues of our life that keep us hung up in the same old destructive patterns.

When I integrated this understanding into my life, pain became my informant. I no longer felt threatened by it because I knew that I could apply my self-care practices to the discomfort and keep the flow of healing happening. I could stay steady in the moment, ride it out, and learn what I needed to learn to let it go. There was no more need to avoid it or numb it. I was stronger now, and I didn't require the instant gratification to get through. I now encouraged discomfort to come forward to help me heal.

When I read about instant gratification in *The Road Less Traveled,* it was one of those moments that felt like a lightbulb had gone off in my head. I understood right away what I had been doing before I found my spiritual practice. It also became clear to me that I didn't have the strength before to look at the sad events of my life, so I instead sought out immediate ways to soothe those feelings when they showed up. I needed to offer myself some feeling of gratification to carry on. My instant gratification methods included finding other people to help and completely investing myself in their recovery so I didn't have to think about my own. Another one was to move faster and get really busy with my career, family, and life in general. I became a perfection addict, making everything—my house, my garden, my appearance—look perfect on the outside while breaking down inside. And I'd avoid situations, people, places, and things that had the potential to hurt me. I felt instant gratification until I didn't. Then like anything that doesn't fill the well of our lives anymore, I started to feel the drought and then the panic because of my inability to truly cope with the feelings that were showing up to be healed.

Revisiting our pain is part of our healing path, and this requires that we learn to sit with suffering and not look for the easy escape. Self-care and meditation practices fortify us to do this. In order to heal through trauma, we have to learn to sit and listen to pain and then wrap our arms around it in gratitude and send it on its way.

LEARNING PATIENCE

Patience is a virtue. What does that mean exactly? To me it's all about the word *virtue.* It's about the importance that we place on being moral, integral, and dignified on the many paths of our life. It suggests to me a measured and purposeful life that is never pressed into reacting in a way that harms you or someone else.

Learning patience is a generous act that soothes your system and brings ease to those around you. In a world that moves at warp speed and is urged to move ever faster, assisting in quieting down your surroundings is a life-support technique that patience supports.

The path to self-realization is a rigorous one. It's made up of thorny, clumsy, sticky, dark experiences. You have tried unsuccessfully to file those experiences away and ignore them, and now you know that can't be done. The only way to lighten their impact is to look them in the eye and address them, otherwise they will gain strength and potentially hurt you more in the future.

In order to really heal, you're going to have to look at the stuff in your life that has interrupted the healing process. This is where patience comes in. Cultivating a patient path allows you to sit with what shows up. Oftentimes it gets tougher before it gets better, and staying the course will depend a lot on the patience and faith you bring to your process. You will rely on your patience to keep you steady so you don't fall into discouragement, which can stop you from moving further down the path of healing. You are strong now, and you can see the obstacles ahead that scared you before but no longer cast that spell on you. You are a spiritual warrior, focused, purposeful, and insightful. You have learned patience, and with that valuable tool you can conquer the darkest, most frightening of obstacles.

ASKING FOR HELP

My inner practice revealed to me many of the roadblocks that had gotten in the way of my healing. I started to notice how truly traumatized I was and how complicated my issues were. This level of self-inquiry guided me to the people I needed to help me heal, and I was led to a psychologist who dealt with my type of trauma. Trust these types of instincts in yourself. If you find you have hit a wall, ask for help and pay close attention to who shows up.

As you become the expert on yourself, you may benefit from the wisdom of others. This is the perfect time to create a support network around you. I call this the healing team. The healing team comes with us on this unique healing journey. Healing is hard work, and resolving to do it all on your own is far too much pressure. The most successful journeys are the ones taken with support and access to your community's resources. A team of professionals can help assess your situation and guide you to practices and people that will support your healing path. It can make all the difference. The list below includes experts I have accessed on my healing journey and that I often recommend to clients.

* Primary care physician and/or naturopathic physician
* 12-Step program with sponsor for those with addiction issues
* Therapist, in particular one specializing in cognitive behavior therapy
* Massage therapist
* Chiropractor
* Yoga instructor or meditation coach (I recommend one with Kundalini yoga and breath expertise)
* Ayurvedic healer
* Specialty therapist, such as art, music, or equine
* Exercise trainer or group exercise program
* Physical therapist
* Light therapist

* EMDR (Eye Movement Desensitization and Reprocessing) therapist
* Acupuncturist

THINKING ABOUT THERAPY

As I was strengthening my awareness and rebuilding my energetic foundation, I noticed issues coming up in my life that I couldn't understand but also couldn't ignore. There was so much anger and sadness appearing that it became difficult to carry on without addressing these emotions. The advice from one of my teachers was clear: seek therapy. I had worked with a psychologist before but had not been ready to do more than use therapy as a way to lessen my extreme levels of anxiety in daily life. This time, after getting in touch with my inner guidance and taking on supportive healing practices, things felt different. I knew that the emotions I was feeling were the portal to greater healing. As scary as they were, I was ready to face them. I understood that if I did not meet these feelings at their source, I would never grow through them.

It was a pivotal time for me and I was able to rebuild as I never had before. I had spent years disassociating from the loss and abandonment of my childhood, and now it was time to look at it with the expertise of a therapist. With his help, I came to understand that my reactions to those difficult events were not shameful or wrong but rather classically appropriate for the trauma I had experienced as a child. I can remember the relief I felt knowing I was no longer alone with these huge emotions. Instead of feeling guilty for my fear, anger, and resentment, I felt validated and understood. I accepted that I could let go of the mean-spirited, doubtful person that I had become because of my hidden pain.

Once I made the decision to see a therapist, my mental burdens lifted and I moved on to discover what parts of my life were calling for healing, validation, and compassion. With each session of therapy I secured trust in my psychologist and let go of the need to figure things out on my own. As noted, working with a therapist helped me to understand that I was not alone. But most important, it helped me validate my feelings and showed me a path to my life that was not available to me before.

Therapy gave me a chance to go to school to study me, Sarah. The coping skills I adopted as a child helped me survive the loss of my parents. But the very skills that had helped me survive the trauma of my childhood were now the root of my suffering in adulthood. To get through the losses, I compartmentalized; I filed away all the sadness, grief, and devastation. Our brains are amazing organs that have the ability to protect us from that which harms us most, but we have to reconnect to the trauma to heal through it. This is what working in therapy helped me do. With each session my awareness grew stronger, less guilty, less shameful, and more proactive.

Unresolved trauma separates us from our happiness and restricts opportunities for us to heal. Pay close attention to the issues in your life that keep appearing. Do they feel similar to issues in the past? It may be that the people and circumstances involved are different but the same emotions and dead-end feelings are brought up. Addressing these feelings with the help of a professional therapist is a beautiful act of self-love.

FINDING A BROADER SENSE OF SELF

Identifying the deep, soulful voice that needs to be heard in us is an important step in nurturing self-awareness. When we transcend the mind's need to define and judge, new worlds open up. Life goes from being one dimensional to fully interactive and connected. Every time you engage your life in an open and compassionate way, you grow in ways that you could hardly conceive of before. You build a relationship with what feeds you and what depletes you, and from that place you become more respectful of your life. You are a part of a greater universe, and all that's needed to get to that place is a commitment to self-healing.

So often we spend time striving for accomplishments in our lives that have nothing to do with our hopes and dreams. We prioritize pleasing our parents, impressing our friends, and satisfying others, all the while losing sight of what really matters to us. We get separated from our true north, our happiness. This can be a slippery slope. There are times when it is appropriate to put the needs of others in front of our own, but if we ignore our own needs for too long, the world around us will get fragile fast!

It is hard to move ahead with a prescribed self-care or meditation practice with a client when she has lost sight of her self-importance and, as a result, her passion and even identity. Sometimes her sense of self is restricted to how she relates to others. She has lost touch with her heart's desire, and she finds herself continually suffering because she is not really doing what she wants to be doing in life. When I ask her what makes her feel good, the answer is "I don't know." In an effort to suppress the parts of us that hurt so much, we numb out our feelings. We all know what this looks like. We move way too fast, busying ourselves to avoid feeling. We drink too much wine, eat too much sugar, smoke. We watch TV in an effort to jump into another reality. We create drama through gossip, blame, and judging others. We participate in hurtful rather than healing actions. It is in this place that our lives feel closed off, restricted, and hopeless.

Self-care gives us the chance to feel stronger about who we are so we can move ahead with the courageous act of self-healing. It is in that place that we start to find a broader sense of who we are and what we have come here to do.

SELF-CARE IS NOT SELF-INDULGENCE

Investing time in self-care might seem like an indulgence or luxury to some people. But I am here to tell you it is a necessity. We live in a time that glorifies overloaded schedules and constant availability. There is a big emphasis on self-sacrifice, especially for women. When we ignore ourselves in an effort to serve others, natural feelings of exhaustion and resentment come up. The emotional upset caused by too much sacrifice provokes a tendency toward anger, resentment, and blame. Self-sacrifice wears us down at every level—physically, emotionally, and spiritually—and puts us in a vicious cycle of suffering. Instead of healing the source of the problem, we treat the symptoms of the suffering, only to repeat the same destructive patterns again. Self-care breaks the cycle. It gives you the strength to discover what you truly need to enrich your life.

You have a purpose in this lifetime, and no one else can do what you have come here to do. Believe that you are worth all the energy it takes to maintain amazing physical, mental, and spiritual health, and that energy will help you to sustain your hopes and dreams. The simple act of self-care will shift your life in ways you never imagined possible. Helping others is an honor when it's offered in a way that honors ourselves first. You are opening the classroom of your life. What support do you need to be the best student possible? This is where we start. Love what is already inside of you. Your precious life awaits you.

START SMALL, GO EASY

The smallest step in the direction of change is a positive step. Wanting things to be different is hopeful but not enough. Setting out to change the environment of your life is vitally important to making a shift that sticks. Doing this can feel very difficult or unattainable; our personal habits and behaviors become deeply ingrained, and the thought of making life changes feels daunting. That is why the changes we implement need to be measured and practiced gently. The end goal is for your life to continue to grow and serve you rather than get you discouraged. To be sustainable, each step should be taken with great consideration.

I have an image of my spirit patiently waiting for me to remember its connection to the mind, body, and heart, and at that magic moment there is a reunion that reminds me that no time has been lost. I've arrived home once again, and all the lessons, trips, and falls it took me to get back home were worth it. This reminds me of something my teacher, Yogi Bhajan, said: "You have to be kind to yourself and you have to forgive your past and you have to have a beautiful tomorrow. The greatest communication is when you communicate with yourself that tomorrow is yours."

UNDERSTANDING THAT THERE IS NO FAILURE

Failure is not a recognized term on a healing journey. Every step you take in the direction of self-love is a step toward awareness and healing. Even if you reach a point where you have to stop, reassess, and start over, nothing is ever lost. Wherever you are in your healing journey, you have developed tools that are yours forever. You have looked thoughtfully and inwardly at the circumstances of your life and have begun a dialogue with yourself that you did not have before. You have rekindled a friendship of the deepest kind, and there will never be another relationship as deep and healing as the one you nurture within yourself.

It is through your love of self that you open the gates not only to your own experience of life and your human nature, but to the entire universe. You have taken important steps, and whatever has come up for you is learning of the best kind.

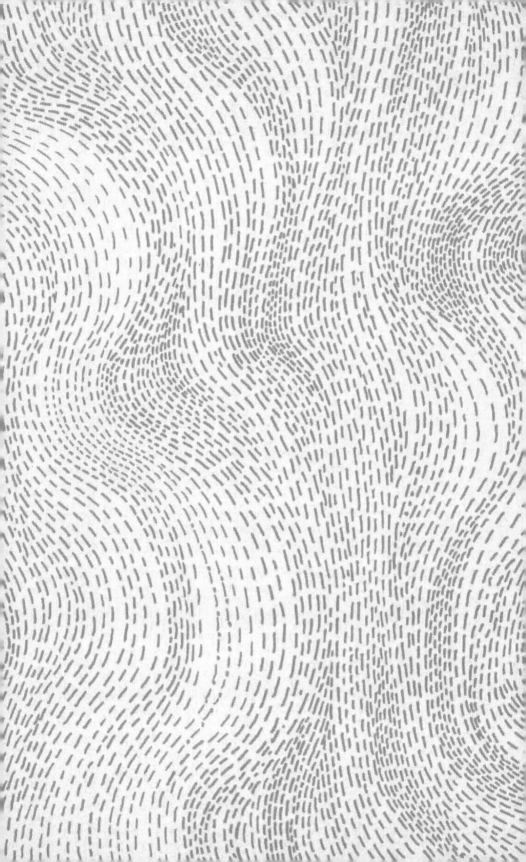

chapter 5

Growing Your Beginner's Mind

WHAT IS A BEGINNER'S MIND?

You are ready to venture out and navigate your way forward on an open-ended trail. There are so many possibilities, and it is this very excitement that will override any discomfort that might come up for you along the way. We fondly call this starting point the beginner's mind. You can bring your beginner's mind to any new experience. With it, opportunities are infinite.

The beginner's mind reminds us of how much there is to learn—and what good news that is. There is nothing to prove and everything to gain. Letting go of old, worn-out information that no longer feels like it's adding quality to your life is a great place to start. How would it feel to unload the burden of *knowing all the things you need to know* about your life and landing in a place that is open and curious about what's ahead? When fear, anxiety, and other negative feelings overwhelm us, there is literally no space in our lives to take in more information. This is the great value of arriving in the beginner's mind. You are a wide-open vessel ready to fill up on new ways of being. You let go of the preconceived notions that have kept you cycling through the same discouraging belief systems. Adopting a beginner's mind can help you take the next steps needed to heal. And when you embrace a beginner's mind, learning flows naturally in and out of you and so much new knowledge is available to you. In the beginner's mind you listen and stay open to the messages of your heart, the sensations of your body, and the truth of your mind. You feel the subtle shifts in your energy and tend to them before they have the potential to throw you off balance and let anxiety take over. This allows you the chance to understand yourself more clearly and take tender care of your life. Every day and every moment is different. The beginner's mind ushers in all possibilities for this fresh start.

EMBRACING YOURSELF AS A BEGINNER

When you embrace yourself as a beginner, there are no restrictions on what can happen. You have the wonder and curiosity of someone starting anew. Children embody the beginner's mind: living in the moment without expectation, not because they are trying to, but because they naturally act that way without the mind's interference. The more we can learn from their example, the better chance we have at living in the moment too.

On this voyage, you'll hold the open-hearted curiosity of a child coupled with the loving protection of a parent. All the choices are yours to make. When you embrace yourself as a beginner, you honor your secret, deep-seated, unheard emotions. You declare yourself ready to break down walls and give voice to the buried, locked-away, frightened feelings, those that are the hardest to access. Emotions that sit below the surface need to be revealed in order to be healed, and the only way to do that is to open up and allow those feelings to arise.

Start from the beginning and offer yourself the chance to learn how to do this one step at a time. Release yourself from the pressure of having to know how to take the next steps alone. Allow me to guide you. All you have to do is show up to participate in the best way you know how.

Each time you engage in the practices of this book, you are growing and healing. Stay steady, patient, and brave, and know that you will be taken care of on this path. Even if you don't feel you're quite there yet, just considering these ideas sends a message to your life that will make you feel stronger. You most likely have heard the saying *Fake it until you make it*. It is very effective when applied to this practice. In a beginner's mind, we let go of preconceived beliefs that have us doubting every step forward. Instead we open our minds to the endless possibilities. Embracing the beginner's mind, even when we don't completely understand what that means, is an act of coming clean with your life and releasing thoughts that have you stuck in the same old patterns so you can start your journey from a fresh, new place.

FEELING YOUR TENDERFEET

The word *tenderfoot* reminds me of the first days of spring, when you go for a walk in bare feet for the first time after many months. Your soles are soft and sensitive, so you take each step carefully, feeling every blade of grass and every pebble below you. You drink up the earth's energy and override the mind's chatter about how much your tender feet hurt because every other sensation is so nurturing.

You continue on because you are so happy to have your feet free, exposed, and connected to something that feels so good. Like life, tenderfeet can feel challenging and rejuvenating at the same time. You love the freedom of taking your first steps, but your tender feet are vulnerable, not yet conditioned for what's ahead. You don't want to hurt yourself, so you take it slowly, all the while knowing that there will be some discomfort, because the mind reminds you of it constantly. But this does not scare you away. You plod on, unwilling to put on shoes because you're driven by something greater, a chance to really feel and be a part of something that feeds your sense of adventure. You are ready for this close connection to the earth, and that far outweighs any of the challenges you have to endure in the process.

Tenderfoot is a starting point, a reset, and the opportunity to experience a beginner's mind again and again. It's an expression of openness, curiosity, and wonder. When we feel the sensations of our life, we are able to act consciously and grow the ability to know what it is we need in the moment. It is through this awareness that we experience life free of the calloused, dysfunctional habits that separate us from what feels best to us. The tenderfoot experience is that reminder to start again. Reset and re- evaluate a way of being that no longer serves a life of learning. When you take your shoes off this spring, notice the impression the earth leaves on your feet. Come back to the care you take of your feet when first you step onto the earth after protecting them from the elements of a harsh winter. Walk forward carefully, knowing that with each step you will get stronger and more connected with your environment and yourself.

PRACTICE: TENDERFOOT JOURNALING

Give yourself some time to digest the concept of tenderfoot and the beginner's mind, as they are important trajectories to the rest of the book. Then take a look at the experiences in your life that embody an open heart and mind and those that make you feel restricted and closed down. When you are ready, pick up your journal and write down your answers to these questions:

1 What does tenderfoot look like in your life?

2 When do you feel you are willing to learn and when do you feel resistant to the lessons in your life?

3 When you are introduced to a new concept, are you willing to learn or do you often feel you already know everything there is to know about it?

4 In your interactions with those closest to you, what triggers you to shut down and go into a protective position and what opens you up and intrigues your curious mind?

Before you close out your journaling for the day, bring back the image of your tenderfeet on the ground so bravely taking the next steps forward. Take six complete deep breaths and hold the image of tenderfoot in your mind. On the final inhale, accept gratitude in your heart for this awareness, and on the final exhale, let go of any judgment that may have come in through this exercise. Trust that everything happens in the most perfect way.

NURTURING YOURSELF AS A CHILD

I love to use the image of a child in describing these initial stages of a practice because for most of us a child's innocence is something we can relate to. When I am near a young child, I feel the urge to hold and cradle her. My guarded, resistant ways relax and I feel myself melt in her precious energy. Being around children helps me understand, even if it is just for a moment, that same kind of innocence in myself.

When we spend time with babies, we are captured by their energy. This is the energy we are trying to capture through the beginner's mind: experiencing what is before us now.

Can you feel that tender place in your heart? Can you experience that same innocence in yourself? It may be masked by years of hurt, anger, and disappointment, but underneath it all there is a child waiting for you.

Think of the wounded parts of you as your child within. You might try looking at a photo of yourself as a baby or child and offering that little one, your inner child, the protection, consideration, and love that you so deserve. What would you do to take care of that child when life got frightening for her? I know what I would do: I'd bend down and look her in the eyes and assure her that I'd take care of her no matter happened. I'd hold her hand, stroke her head, and listen to her concerns.

What if every time fear and anxiety showed up for you, you recognized it as your child? Instead of shielding yourself from the sadness and discomfort, you turn toward it and offer it a soft touch, giving it more love and less criticism. Mindfulness gives you the chance to observe your feelings before you get all rolled up in them.

Life's energy is always calling us home, and home is that tender place within where everything can be sorted out. There is such value in deep listening. Hear your body, your heart, your mind, and your spirit and see what feels right, what feels wrong, what feels empowering, and what feels painful. Learn to listen and feel, and use this information to grow compassion for yourself and make loving choices for your life.

BEING KIND TO YOURSELF

Some of the kindest people I know use harsh, cruel language when talking about themselves. The very same people wouldn't think of using this type of language in describing another person, and yet they speak so carelessly about themselves. I feel the urge to protect people when I hear them talking in this way. Speaking negatively about ourselves broadcasts a message to the world that we are not worthy of love, respect, and compassion. When we disrespect who we are, it makes sense that others would do the same. When we speak negatively about ourselves, it's as though we are trying to talk others out of loving us. We all yearn to be loved, respected, and honored, and that reality starts in loving ourselves first. If you do not have the ability to cherish your own life, it will be hard to help others feel that love and respect for you.

A big part of self-care is listening to what we say to ourselves. If we have a healthy regard for the life we are leading, others will also have respect for us. Acknowledging yourself as both teacher and beginner or parent and child invites the frightened, wounded part of yourself to come out from behind the shadow and move beyond the restrictions that trauma has brought to your life.

BRINGING AWARENESS INTO YOUR LIFE

When we pay attention to our words and understand the power they have on us and others, we change our life completely.

Some books find you at the perfect time and open up your mind to these realizations in the best possible way. For me, one of those books was *The Four Agreements* by Don Miguel Ruiz. In it, Ruiz proposes four essential rules to guide your personal behavior. His ideas are so simple, yet so very powerful. The rule *Be impeccable with your word* on the surface seems to mean to be honest. Digging deeper, his idea of being impeccable is more than telling the truth. It means that everything you say must be a good representation of who you are. For example, do you consider yourself a compassionate person? Then your words naturally come from a place of compassion. No gossip, no rumors, no criticism—of others or of yourself. Ruiz's book challenged me to bring awareness to every word I spoke. We all have habits we've learned and practiced for most of our lives; some of them are healthy conscious habits and others keep us locked in destructive behaviors and ways of thinking. The following practice addresses these habits.

PRACTICE: SELF-KINDNESS

In this practice I ask you to consider your voice as a powerful tool. Understand that everything you say has an impact on your life personally and exponentially. Your voice can be used to harm or to heal. How will you use your voice?

Part 1

1 Only say positive things to yourself and others today. When you speak, notice the quality and intention of what you are saying and ask yourself how it serves you and those around you.

2 Use kind words or stay quiet.

3 Watch people as you speak kindly to them; notice their body language and how grateful they are, and then notice how this makes you feel inside.

Part 2

1 Look in the mirror and give yourself a compliment. Look at your eyes—notice the color, the shape, and the expression they hold.

2 If you look tired or sad, bless yourself with hope and encouragement.

3 Close your eyes and visualize the healthiest, happiest version of yourself. Feel gratitude as you inhale and wash yourself in gratitude, and on the exhale release any negativity this exercise brings up for you.

4 Finish with "I love you."

NOTICING FRIENDSHIPS BUILT ON WOUNDS

When we reinforce our insecurities by getting someone else's negative acknowledgment of the pain and injustice of the event, it reinforces and strengthens the pain inside us. In friendship it is natural to look to others who have dealt with similar painful circumstances, especially when we haven't dealt with our own negative habits and fears. Caroline Myss, a renowned expert in human conciousness, calls this interchange the language of woundology: you build social circles with people who have similar experiences to normalize what is going on for you.

Here's an example: a person suffering from the devastation of divorce looks to others who have had marital problems or are divorcing too. Conversations can embody blame, regret, anger, and even revenge. In a wounded state, it is easy to seek out like-minded people who would rather talk about their wounds and their perceived injustices than do anything about them.

If this coping mechanism is a familiar one, you don't have to rush out and cut off your social ties with certain people, but be aware of how you feel when you are with them. Make decisions about how you will steer the conversations to feel more productive, and if that can't happen, set boundaries on what you will tolerate. As you begin to heal and get stronger, you won't be drawn to these kinds of conversations or people any longer. Inevitably your awareness will shift the relationship's energy and there will be little interest for you to continue taking part in these blame-filled conversations.

Early in my healing journey, I had a hard time letting go of these dysfunctional friendships. I'd keep trying to find a connection or overlook a glaring reality about a certain person and our situation together. These efforts were always discouraging and inevitably brought on further sadness. Finally I started to accept the signs and let go of the struggle. My faith became stronger than my fear about the loss. I surrendered to what was in front of me while feeling a deep gratitude for each of the lessons these people and situations delivered to me.

Remember that these relationships served you when you were weak. You came into each other's lives for a reason, and sometimes you make the shifts in perspective together and the friendships grow from the learning you've done together. But when this doesn't happen, understand that you have learned what you needed to learn from one another and now it is time to move on.

THE HONEYMOON PERIOD

The first few stages of creating a healing practice are wonderful. They're considered a honeymoon period. This is the time when you first discover how incredible it feels to find yourself. Your life has delivered you to this time and place to do exactly what you are doing and you feel all the support around you. Paulo Coelho says in *The Alchemist,* "all the universe conspires to make it happen." You have felt a hunger for something bigger in your life, and you have found what you were looking for. Your spirit has been calling out, and now that the call has been heard and answered, you are rejoicing in the practice you have developed. There is so much to celebrate about that! You feel loved and supported, and now you begin an intense journey of self-discovery. But just like the euphoric feelings of falling in love with another person, it takes hard work to keep that connection. That's the difficult part. Many people long to maintain the euphoria, but euphoria is not a sustainable emotion, and it's only natural that the intensity of that feeling would lessen over time. It's not realistic, or even healthy, to stay in a place of such intensity—that would be an out-of-balance emotional state. It is healthy to enjoy the honeymoon period, but it is more important to your long-term success to get real with the discipline of the practice. The ultimate goal is to find an enduring, strong sense of contentment, not a quick fix.

There is such incredible relief when the healing process begins, and it's a natural tendency to want to help those you love. You want the whole world to know! But do your best to resist that temptation, at least initially.

After connecting clients with a meditation practice, very often they say to me, "Why doesn't *everyone* do this?!" There is no denying how satisfying it is to find the practice that speaks to you so deeply, and as a generous person, it's only natural that you'd want your loved ones to feel the same comfort. Sharing is a beautiful gesture, but doing so in the honeymoon stage can put your commitment to the practice in jeopardy. Also keep in mind that recruiting someone else to follow your lead robs that person of the opportunity to be called to the practice by their spirit.

The honeymoon period is an important part of a spiritual journey and is yours alone to experience. If you drag someone else into the practice, that person misses out on the call-and-fulfillment experience. Likewise, his or her devotion to the practice won't be as strong as yours, and that person might actually walk away from the practice when the exercises get challenging. It can be a negative experience, and it puts too much pressure on everyone involved. The most important thing that you can do is to be responsible for yourself. Isn't that asking plenty, anyway?

Help others by living mindfully. Devote yourself to your inner study, and allow those around you to naturally benefit from the positive changes that are happening to you. The impact of your actions is so much more powerful than mere words. Words are empty when they are not backed by committed action. Stay the course and allow your new way of being to become familiar and stable to you first. When those around you see your life shifting, they may be inspired to look at their own lives too.

PRESERVING YOUR ENERGY

Right now, you need every ounce of energy you have to stay steady in your practice. That means focusing on your own experience, not someone else's. You don't yet fully grasp the ways in which the practice will shape your life. By directing your focus and energy away from yourself and trying to involve or teach others, you deflect your focus from yourself.

Become as deeply honest with yourself as possible. This is a time for internal focus, not external advocacy. When you have an impulse to "go public" with your new practice, stop and ask yourself where that impulse comes from and what it would feel like to take the focus away from yourself right now.

When I started to feel the first shifts, I wanted to go out and tell everyone how incredible it felt, but I didn't have the words. This helped me stay inward. The shifts that appear initially may be more apparent than those that happen as you progress. This work is potent but so often subtle in how it affects us. This is a good time to reinforce your commitment to change. This is a process of laying a foundation for self-care that will support you for the rest of your life. Once you make room for this new lifestyle, it will be as though you opened a faucet of healing for your life. The fire you feel is there to ignite that part of you that has been hidden, and this newfound awareness is a gift. But take it slowly, or you'll find yourself lost on the trail of self-care. We need to assure our commitment to ourselves first or the healing process will not be sustainable. When difficult times hit, it's instinctual to want to feel better *now,* but building a spiritual foundation takes a commitment and discipline that will be with you for the rest of your life. This is something far more profound and permanent than anything immediate gratification can ever offer you.

PRACTICE: MORNING REFLECTION

This practice is a gentle introduction to meditation. It does not take on the structure of a sitting practice but helps you release the urgency of jumping out of bed before taking time to reflect. It will give you an understanding of how important it is to pause before losing yourself in any activity. It will connect you with the vital systems of your life, your breath, your heartbeat, and the energy of your navel center. Don't underestimate the potency of this simple practice! Devote yourself to it and journal your discoveries. You'll be amazed at how much you'll learn.

1 In the morning before you get out of bed, lay still and place your right hand on your heart and your left hand on your belly. Breathe deeply, filling your lungs and expanding your torso as you inhale and pulling your navel back to your spine as you exhale, emptying your lungs. Notice your breath. Does it flow easily? Is there any restriction? If so, where in the body do you feel the restriction? How does taking this time feel to you? What ideas float into your head as you breathe? What emotions fill you? Practice this for six rounds of breath (an inhale and an exhale counts as one round) before you get out of bed.

2 Swing your legs over the bed, letting your feet either dangle or rest on the ground. Pay attention to the lengthening of your spine. It is important to have a strong, lengthened spine to support the energy in your body so you can feel the healing benefits of this breathing exercise.

3 Visualize a place that makes you feel safe, centered, and grounded, like in the Finding a Safe Place Within practice on page 58. Bring three more rounds of breath to that feeling of safety. You may visualize what that place looks like, or it might just be a feeling. Whatever it is, fully experience what shows up. Close your eyes, place your hands on your heart, and give gratitude to yourself for making time in your day to do this practice.

Practice this every day for a week and notice the difference it makes in your life. Note the benefits and the struggles you encounter in your journal. If you feel ready for it, keep going with the practice beyond the week, with the ultimate goal of completing the practice every morning for forty days in a row.

BECOMING VULNERABLE, OPENING UP

Everything about your life has brought you to this moment. There are parts, even the difficult experiences, that we see as gifts to our journey, and there likely are parts you are ready to leave behind so you can make room for what is to come. Honor the old ways of being, and excuse them from your life now. The first steps without the old "security blanket" may feel wobbly, but you'll make it through as long as you add loving practices to take their place.

As you practice with dedication and loyalty, you will feel liberated, empowered, receptive, and happy, but you will also feel vulnerable at times. This will be particularly true after you have moved through the honeymoon stage of your practice. When you start to hit your stride with your commitment to the practices, things happen rapidly. You have given your spirit the signal that you are ready to heal old wounds. It is during this time, more than likely, that there will come a day when you feel quite intimidated, naked, and unprepared for the memories that reappear. This is entirely normal. Come back to the ease and simplicity of the beginner's mind and let it support you. Meet your challenges with curiosity and confidence. Be aware of your old ways of coping so you don't get trapped in deep-rooted behaviors. There may be some coping behaviors that still help you, so be clear with yourself which ones they are when they show up. Ask yourself if they still feel supportive to your life. If not, be willing to let them go.

Vulnerability is an open state. No matter how exposed you feel, you are safe in the present moment. When you see yourself as vulnerable, you have the greatest chance to grow. Not every moment of vulnerability will make you feel fragile—on the contrary, when you embrace the state of openness that comes with vulnerability, you will start to know a different level of learning and growth. If you put up walls every time fear creeps in, no learning will happen, because you have barricaded yourself from your vulnerability. If you run every time you're confused, fearful, or anxious, you will never find clarity, and you will grow weary trying to outrun your feelings. If you hide your vulnerability from the world, the world will sense your resistance and you will lose the chance to connect with others and possibly miss the support of people who could be vitally important to your journey. Take small steps into the unchartered territory of vulnerability and notice how much you grow when you turn toward that which frightens you most.

Dysfunctional coping mechanisms are part of the wardrobe of clothes that we wear and vulnerability is stark nakedness. I look down and see that some clothes no longer fit. They are uncomfortable. They cover me; they do the basic job of getting me through the day, but I have outgrown them. I can picture the new clothes that will fit soon, but first I need to shed my old clothes. When I remove those clothes, I am naked. I am bare and vulnerable. It is risky, but it is also healing. Only by becoming naked can I put on the new clothes of my new life, clothes that will make me understand who I am more clearly. These clothes fit me beautifully. I have hand-picked them on my healing journey, and I benefit from my new wardrobe.

LISTENING TO YOUR HEART

You are inspired to change your life. You feel excited about it in your body. You're ready to open your heart to this new path. Your thoughtful mind is working hard to fit new ideas into old ways of thinking. You have also learned that sometimes the ego gets in the way. Even with the best intentions, the ego fears change and failure and will encourage self-sabotage. Be aware of this. Old behaviors don't let go of us easily and soon become burdensome to our life. Sometimes these acts of sabotage even look like really good ideas at the time!

This is why cultivating the ability to check into the deepest parts of who we are is so valuable. Listen to your heart: it will burn through the antics of a sneaky ego. When in doubt, get quiet, go inside, and ask your heart for guidance. It will never let you down. Your heart is your absolute truth and will be there to advise you. The more we strengthen our connection to the heart, the more we trust the advice that it offers us. The beginner's mind is a beautiful place because it is full of potential. Now it's time to take the humility and eagerness of the beginner's mind and put it into action.

chapter 6

Cultivating the Witness in You

So far you have worked to put yourself back in touch with the energy of your body, made space in your life for quiet reflection, and encouraged your heart to send its messages of truth. You are once again finding wonder at the beauty of the world around you. Through journaling, noticing your behavior, and meditation, you have started to tap into the inner experiences of your life. You have encouraged and supported this part of yourself like you would a small child and have listened for her voice to speak up. From this foundation of gentle self-care, we can now move to some of the more advanced elements of this journey. The time has come to go deeper.

THE STORM AND THE OBSERVER

I have lived my entire life in New England, so I have had many opportunities to watch storms roll in. What starts as cloud cover soon turns into dark skies, high winds, and some form of powerful precipitation. A storm is an extreme example of energy that wields a huge amount of power over our lives and environment. Storms devour the shores with wind, high tides, rain, and cold, and then lift and clear just as suddenly. They knock down trees, rip out electric lines, blow ships onto the shore, and wash out roads. In just a matter of minutes, there can be incredible destruction and even loss of life. It can happen so quickly and disappear as abruptly as it arrived, but the damage can last for a lifetime.

I was much like a storm before I cultivated a practice of self-care. Out of a clear blue sky, I could be seized by panic or anger, and without a safe haven to observe these emotions, they would flood in, making me feel fragile and unsafe in my own life. I would get caught in all that was before me and react to the circumstances rashly, which would inevitably bring embarrassment, regret, and sadness in the aftermath. Relationships would be harmed, lovely plans destroyed, and my body would ache from the stress of it all.

Like the extreme energy unleashed by a severe storm, my whole life would get stirred up by my fury, despair, panic, and fear. Rather than learning how to take care of myself in these moments, I tried to lock my emotions away, which caused further destructive behavior, like a hurricane erupting into a life that was calm and peaceful just moments before. Later I could see that these storms were indicator lights guiding me to pay attention to my body's energetic system, which had fallen out of balance.

Connecting my emotional outbursts to the weather gave me the perspective I needed. For example, when I watch a storm blowing in from the ocean, I have two choices: I can watch it from the safety of my home while assessing what will need to be taken care of later; or I can go outside to try to manage the damage as it happens, putting myself in danger of being tossed around by the wind and rain. I was always at the mercy of the unpredictable weather of my emotions, and I needed to find a way to seek shelter and deal with the aftereffects of the storm.

DETECTING THE STORM INSIDE US

When panic is triggered, adrenaline rushes into our body, alerts our mind, and has us reacting to an event, consciously or subconsciously, in one way or another. Sometimes these events are worthy of immediate reaction, but oftentimes they are not. It only takes a millisecond of an anxiety response to throw the world into a tailspin. In this case, the storm is happening inside your own body, mind, and spirit. Your emotional storms might involve saying something you wish you had never said or doing something to someone that you now regret. Or maybe your history of rash decisions in the heat of the moment has caused all sorts of problems for you and others.

When we become the storm, we put ourselves and those around us in emotional jeopardy. It feels out of control, because it is.

You know you're in an emotional storm when:

* You take the actions of others personally
* You are constantly overwhelmed but don't take steps to do something about it
* You are afraid of difficult conversations, so you aren't truthful about your feelings
* You can't believe how much anger certain events trigger in you
* You avoid certain people and situations because you do not know how to put healthy boundaries around your relationships
* You feel lost and frustrated with your life but take no action to change anything

BECOMING THE OBSERVER

When a storm rips through your emotional life, don't just go through the motions: scrutinize the causes and effects by becoming the observer. Unlike the weather outside, we can stand back and decide whether we'll become the storm or be the observer of the storm.

After the storm has settled, notice what you do. Is it your tendency to pick up the pieces by blaming others for your anger? Or do you take complete responsibility for your actions? Whatever the case, every storm requires some damage control, and how you handle it matters. If you recognize and regret your actions, you are already instinctively moving in a direction of self-healing. Reflecting on the disorder instead of deflecting it is a powerful step in the right direction. This is a step toward accountability and healing your life. You are becoming the observer, the person who reads the signs and pauses before reacting to the situation. You rest in the deepest parts of your being and watch the storm from a distance before going in to try to resolve whatever has been stirred up.

Becoming the observer means being aware of how we think, what we say, and how we react to the circumstances of life. Becoming the observer diffuses the anxiety in any situation and helps us respond in a way that makes us feel safe and strong. When we can step away from the emotional experiences of life, just for a moment, shifts of awareness happen. These shifts allow us to be more generous in our actions. We begin to see our thoughts through a different lens, a more compassionate one that nurtures nonjudgment and allows us to be accountable. From there, we respond to life in a thoughtful and deliberate manner.

At first, becoming the observer will help you realize that a storm is happening, and over time you will naturally begin to notice how you feel when the storm is present in your life. You will get better at detecting when a storm is gathering. This awareness alone will make room in your life to make choices that weren't possible before. And soon you will be able to prevent those storms from wreaking havoc on your life. You will read the signs and take precautions to make yourself feel safe and you will channel your energy into healthy awareness instead of unleashing storms of anger, blame, or panic.

You become the observer when:

* You find a strong self-care practice that nurtures yours strengths and weaknesses
* You know how to find your center in the most difficult situations
* You learn how to breathe mindfully and use your breath throughout the day as needed to respond to stressful situations
* You find compassion and forgiveness for other people's shortcomings and see the situation from all points of view
* You create safe perimeters around difficult people and situations in your life
* You do not get sucked into stress-filled interactions and instead keep a healthy perspective

PRACTICE:
SEEING LIFE THROUGH THE OBSERVER LENS

Does the awareness of the storm and observer make you feel unsettled? Does it ignite the storm in you, or are you comfortable with this understanding? Whatever the case may be, just asking the question directs your attention inward, and that is the purpose of every practice. With this practice you'll ease into the experience of being the observer and notice life from a spacious perspective.

— TO DO THE PRACTICE —

At the beginning of the day, identify situations that might allow you to step back and observe what is going on in a different way. You do not have to physically step back; just try to observe and listen with a new level of awareness.

In your moments of quiet reflection, begin viewing your life as though you were watching it on a movie screen. Instead of responding to what you see, hear, and feel with judgment, be in the moment with what is before you. Notice the details of what's going on and allow the information to flow through your senses instead of getting tangled in opinions about what appears. Be curious.

When the "movie" is over, do you like what you have seen? How could you best support the situation? Take time to journal your feelings about what appeared and how it felt to look at life in this way. How did it feel to let the events flow through you instead of analyzing and having an opinion on everything that happened? What surprised you or provoked some other emotional reaction?

When you see your life through the lens of the observer, you start to feel like you are in partnership with the universe. That is the truth of our lives. We are never alone, but anxiety, fear, and suffering can absolutely make us feel that way. So now instead of fending off what life brings to you, how about turning toward that ever-present energy and recognizing that you are the common denominator in all the events of your life?

WHO ARE YOU WHEN NOBODY'S WATCHING?

How do you behave when you are alone? Just because there is no one around, do you feel there are no real consequences? You can act seemingly without repercussions many times a day. You can make decisions that probably won't impact your reputation or get you into real trouble. It's like a secret only you know. For example, if you vent your frustration by speaking unkindly to a stranger without any witness present, does it really matter? If you throw trash out the window when you're alone in the car or slide a small item into your pocket at the store and don't get caught, are these really crimes? If you sneak in foods that aren't on your diet, is it really cheating? What about when the sneaking extends to alcohol, drugs, or sex outside of your relationship? If nobody important to you finds out, does it really count?

Who we are when nobody is watching counts just as much as when we are around others. In a way it counts more. Just invite the observer to come take a look, and notice the uncomfortable feelings that come up. The observer is spirit, the higher self, the soul, the universe, nature, and God. The observer urges us to take responsibility for how we live. It is our moral compass and can guide the journey of our life. It is a gift to observe the many ways we interact with life and all the possibilities that exist as a result.

So the question is, "Who are you when nobody's watching?" Do your actions match up with the behavior you admire in yourself and in others? If you feel compelled to act one way in public and another way in private, ask yourself why. If you are keeping certain behaviors and actions secret, what are the real consequences?

The answers to these questions may not be easy to look at, but when you inquire with sincerity, concern, and responsibility, you become empowered in a whole new way. You relate to life not as a victim, with life rolling over you, but as a proactive hero. You no longer react first and regret later. The observer asks questions of you that you dared not answer before. You take responsibility for all your interactions and start to let go of the habits and behaviors that do more harm than good.

This level of inquiry is a big order, one that requires that you take it slowly so you can build a strong foundation. The first step is to spend time thinking about ways of strengthening, enlivening, and restoring your ability to have a happy life. Pay attention to what you are doing when nobody is watching and note your discoveries in your journal.

UNDERSTANDING THE LAW OF KARMA

When I began to cultivate a strong relationship with the observer, I stopped moving through life mindlessly. It became clear to me how powerful my thoughts were and how powerful my responses to those thoughts could be. I noticed how mindful thoughts reinforced positive outcomes. What happens when we channel our lives in positive ways rather than in an unconscious way? What I discovered was that outrageously wonderful things happen.

This realization helped me further understand the law of karma, the theory of cause and effect. Karma is a word that is thrown around a lot these days. Even when it's not used in the context of the yogic tradition, people generally understand that the concept references the spiritual consequences of real-world decisions. Karma tells us that our actions have the power to help and hurt ourselves and others. How you treat the circumstances of your life now will impact the lessons and experiences you have in the future. If your actions are fair, kind, and respectful, your life will deliver back the same type of honor. And if you are able to face the difficult challenges of your life with respect and grace, you will be held in that energy during your life. If your actions feel careless and hurtful, your lessons will deliver hurtful experiences that will mirror back that hurt to you in your life.

As the observer, karma explains that our actions pave the way for future experiences. If we are stuck in a cycle of negative patterns, our future experiences will be affected by these cycles of suffering. The destructive thought processes will ultimately feed us back the same experiences and the same sadness. This is when life can get burdensome and exhausting. The circumstances may look different than they did before, but they trigger the same emotions and reactions in us.

Karma helps us understand the concept of accountability in our lives: your thoughts, your words, your actions, and your relationships. Karma acknowledges that there is give and take in the universe. There is a greater energy that's interacting with our lives, not sometimes but all the time. We may not be able to see it with our eyes or touch it with our hands, but it is always there.

Becoming the observer makes it easy to identify our thoughts and actions and enables us to get ahead of the cycle of suffering. We become mindful and purposeful in our actions. When we turn our focus, power, and knowledge inward, the observer allows us to create new patterns of positive energy that bring happiness into our lives.

FINDING THE COMMON DENOMINATOR

My world was rocked when my observer brought a certain realization to light for me: all of the hurtful situations I had experienced throughout my young life, in different places and with different people, had one common denominator, *me*. Every heartbreak in my life had one thing in common: it was *my* heart that broke. I couldn't run away from the fact that it was I who tied all these experiences together. Up until then, I'd do anything to avoid responsibility for what happened when difficulty showed up.

Blame is an easy default reaction to difficulty. In fact, playing the blame game is a go-to behavior that all of us have adopted at one time or another. This action of putting responsibility entirely on someone else for the challenges that show up in life may ease the burden of immediate suffering for a short while, but it has us missing the valuable lessons of owning our part in what happened. And it makes life far more challenging in the long run.

By accepting the observer's knowledge, the opportunities to open ourselves up to healing and growth multiply. You find strength in moments of doubt and weakness. Unlike the helpless perspective of the victim, the observer reveals many solutions. Victimhood keeps us trapped in the same tired cycles and drains us of our energy, but the observer provides us with a chance to reset and rebalance our lives once and for all.

When I started to consider the karmic energy I was projecting into the world, I knew I needed to pay more attention to my actions and behaviors. My life had been feeding me situations that triggered deeper feelings and initiated reactions based on old wounds. I started wondering what would happen if I took ownership of these situations and focused on the source of the pain so I could heal through it. What if I took control instead of watching life from the sidelines? If I really accepted that the observer was guiding me, I had the chance to change my position from victim to empowered hero.

I learned that I couldn't change the outer world, but I could change my behavior and my reactions to the events that appeared. There were ways to heal my thoughts, change my actions, and plan for my dreams. Self-love became my life's primary force. I knew that without self-love, no other healing practice had a chance of helping me heal my life.

The beautiful thing was that my observer showed me the ways in which I was the common denominator in all of the *good* parts of my life too. Creating my wonderful family. Making friends feel loved and safe. Working hard at my studies and my job. Being a thoughtful, kind person in my daily life. The observer reminded me that I was doing a lot of things right.

I once heard it described this way: when you don't accept full responsibility for your life, it is as though you are watching a movie and don't like what you see on the screen. You may want to walk up to the screen and remove the villain, but you know that's impossible. The only power you have is in changing the lens that plays the movie. *You* are the one factor in your life that is always present. So doesn't it make sense to hone your strengths, create clarity, and bring honor into the life you lead?

STEPPING AWAY FROM BLAME

Blame and panic are intricately bound together. They both have a relationship with fear. When we don't have the strength to truly own our thoughts, regrets, and sadness, we act out in ways that are not true to our nature. We say things we don't mean to say and resent people and situations when we don't speak up for ourselves. It all gets very complicated and dramatic. In fear, we blame others because we are fearful of what they would think of us if they knew how we really felt inside. It is natural to want to portray ourselves in the best light possible, but when this is done at the expense of others, suffering continues.

Blame is a slippery slope. There are many circumstances in life in which people feel justified in blaming another, and it is not the purpose of this book to try to convince you otherwise. Only you will know if it is time to heal through blame. Ask yourself how holding on to blame is affecting your life. I'm not asking you to forget the situations that have hurt you, only to be truthful about how holding on to them is affecting your physical, emotional, and spiritual life. Are you strengthened by this blame? Are you enlightened by this anger? Are you revitalized by your resentment? If the answer is yes to any of these questions, then it's not yet time to do this work. That knowledge is just as valuable as anything else you know about yourself.

When we come into deep relationship with ourselves, we become responsible for the events of our life. We don't carelessly fling our energy around anymore, acting in ways that don't align with our true spirit. When we stay present with what is before us and are conscious of our words and actions, life becomes simpler and drama drops away. There is far less damage control and excuses to make for why things didn't turn out the way you had hoped. A natural loving flow to life shows up.

Self-care practices have given me the ability to distinguish blame and discernment in my life. Awareness-focused practices such as Finding a Safe Place Within (page 58), Self-Kindness (page 83), and the Introductory Meditation (page 155) help make me an active observer in my life. When I trip up and act unconsciously now, I am so very grateful for the observer's perspective. I have the chance to apologize and take ownership for my lack of awareness.

Many of us blame unconsciously, and for some people the cycle will never end. We could rely on blame as a coping mechanism forever, but does it get us further down the path of healing or does it just recycle the same pain that makes us suffer even more intensely every time we try to escape that pain through blame? If you've picked up this book, you've already taken important steps in breaking this disempowering cycle. Awareness combined with personal ownership and a disciplined practice will set you free from blame.

OWNING IT ALL

When you take responsibility for what you attract to your life, you learn how to blow the clouds away and welcome the sun. But you must own your *whole* life, not just portions of it. This is personal ownership. If you have been drawn to this book, I suspect you already have some understanding about personal ownership. Even if you haven't heard of the phrase before, you might be seeking it all the same. Questioning your role in the cycle of trauma is an act of personal ownership. Reading a book about self-care is an act of self-love. Self-love asks you to take a truthful look at the whole picture, to bravely take in the less-than-perfect parts of yourself that are asking for change.

Ownership means understanding the difference between your ego's will and the will of the observer, guided by the universe, God, or whatever speaks to you. Here are qualities of the two:

Ego energy:

* controlled   * unsuccessful   * disappointing

* manipulated   * stuck

Observer energy:

- flowing
- organic
- spontaneous
- accepting
- open
- joyful

Take time to listen deeply to what you feel when aggravation or disruption shows up. It could be someone honking at you from behind for no apparent reason or an unsettling phone call from a loved one. No matter what it looks like, embrace it all. Notice your reaction to what happens. Do you immediately go to blame? Or do you stay open? Do you question the part you played in the uncomfortable situation?

Owning it all takes courage and endurance. It means being present in life and setting blame aside. This practice comes with the understanding that every challenge shows up with a lesson that can be learned. I love the chance to work with this concept as often as possible, and particularly in situations where I feel the greatest challenges.

PRACTICE: STOP, LOOK, AND LISTEN

I have been working with the concept of the observer for most of my career, and I have found one of the most effective techniques to grasp it is something I call Stop, Look, and Listen. This practice will help you call on the observer and teach you to pause before addressing any alarming circumstances.

— TO DO THE PRACTICE —

1 **Stop.** When the observer in you recognizes that something is triggering you, it's time to hit the pause button. Take the power of the moment back for yourself. Sometimes this means literally excusing yourself from a situation, stepping into the bathroom, getting off the phone. You will learn respectful ways of doing this. Be kind in your actions and you will discover how easily you can move through discomfort when it appears. Be alone and still for a moment. Experience what has appeared and activate the Long Deep Breath (page 129) to help you feel space.

2 **Look.** Take a fresh look at the situation from other perspectives, beyond just your own gut reaction. This can be the most difficult part of the practice. We have been reacting to trigger situations the same way for a very long time, so the brain will instinctively want to go back to that reactive state. Stand strong and guide yourself toward the view of the observer. Observing deeply before reacting guides the brain in another direction. It sends the message that you are choosing a calmer way of dealing with the situation. The trigger itself matters less than your awareness. Look at everything—the physical, emotional, mental, and spiritual—from the triggered state. Deeply feel what this experience has brought up for you. Do your best, and take as much time as you need before moving on.

3 **Listen.** This is the part of the exercise that cultivates your relationship with the observer. You ask yourself, "What do I do next?" This is the opportunity to trust what comes through and know that it comes from a far more compassionate and generous place than what the ego would offer. How you proceed now will change your experience. When you see changes in your actions, you will feel encouraged and motivated to keep up. Soon you will find yourself guided more instinctively to this way of coping.

Understand that most situations do not demand an urgent response. Life is not an emergency. By slowing down the reactionary process, we have time to heal old, destructive cycles of behavior, gently start to release trauma, and experience the portal of happiness that is our true birthright. Stop, look, and listen and become an expert at healing your life with grace.

GUIDING THE EGO WITH THE OBSERVER

The unconscious ego is an instrument of fear, and untamed it brings continual suffering to life. But what I haven't yet talked about is how essential the conscious ego is in our lives. We cannot live without the ego. It is the brain, the mind, and the center for what we know mentally and how we function and live our lives. But when it is not guided by the balanced energy of the observer, the ego acts on the fearful triggers of the mind instead of the poised, graceful expressions of heart and spirit.

If the ego's moments of out-of-control rage and panic are storms, then the observer exposes us to a view of the storm from above. The observer guides us to safety and warns us of the challenges the storm that is the ego could play on our lives. I have found that the more I practice self-care, self-love, and meditation, the more I am able to identify when the unconscious, fearful ego is at play in my life instead of the expansive, soothing perspective of the observer. It becomes easy to distinguish the two. One way of noticing is that it takes so much more effort and energy to live in the unconscious ego than the conscious ego. With the observer there is a clarity and strength to the experience that is not present otherwise.

This insight of the observer may come to you through your meditation practice initially or spontaneously through everyday activities. But when it is activated in your life, you know it. It's an intuitive, wise energy that doesn't come with a lot of fanfare. Its wisdom has a greater purpose than that of the immediate decision or the attached outcome. The observer helps us let go of taking life so personally, and this takes the pressure off of the difficult situations in our lives.

NURTURING THE OBSERVER WITH SELF-CARE

My new relationship with self-awareness came with a lot of responsibility. Truthfully, at times, I didn't know if I was up for the task of owning what I had to own. Sometimes I wondered if I could just go back to being unaware, living life in the unconscious, haphazard way I had before I came into relationship with the observer. Life with storms was chaotic and disruptive, but it was what I knew. It was familiar. But I soon realized that going back was no longer an option. Instead, when I felt the disruptive triggers, I gathered the information and turned my attention toward the fear that showed up, no longer choosing distraction or overreaction. I stopped pushing away overwhelming feelings; I recognized them for what they were and embraced them like I would a child in need.

Self-care was no longer a choice; it was a requirement for my health and well-being. It was the only way I would be able to sustain this path of healing. I began to see that I also owed it to the people I loved to feel happier. I started to embrace my hopes and dreams instead of managing the disorder that my pain delivered. I started giving in deep and nurturing ways, and when I felt depleted, I'd pause and take care of myself with yoga, meditation, clean eating, and rest. I could feel my world opening up. Everything became available to me in this joyful place.

Positivity felt good inside. Negativity only brought more negative trials and ultimately misery to my life. Have you ever met an unhappy person who was truly successful at all levels: physical, emotional, mental, and spiritual? Inner happiness became an absolute requirement for doing the greater work of life. So the important question was how do I make myself feel loved, safe, and happy? It was through self-care and self-love. I wanted a chance at life that wasn't burdened by the restrictions that my unresolved trauma had placed on me. This was an attainable goal! For my relationships and experiences to be healthy and genuine, it required that I take extraordinary care of myself. From there I had a chance, finally, to move on.

MOVING AHEAD

It is vital to take a step back from time to time and assess how the changes you've made feel in your life. We've learned how valuable change is to healing. Without it there is no way of moving ahead on a healing path. But equally as important is understanding how much energy is required to sustain these changes. Not every day will be easy! You will need to be gentle with yourself, and utilizing the observer's eye to gauge how you are doing will help you take great care of yourself as you move ahead. The success of your hard work is dependent on this knowledge. The observer has the ability to guide you in ways that the ego does not, and with this awareness your world opens up in expansive ways, offering you infinite possibilities to heal your life.

chapter 7

Making Space for the Sacred

▬ ▬ ▬ ▬ ▬ ▬ ▬ ▬ ▬ ▬ ▬ ▬ ▬ ▬ ▬ ▬ ▬ ▬ ▬

You are sacred. This is a powerful statement, and each of us will react to it in a different way. You might be ready to believe these words. If you feel hesitation, though, you're not alone. When we struggle with emotions like anxiety, depression, fear, and resentment, we can feel anything but sacred. I believe that every person has something precious inside of him or her. This is what connects us to the energy of the universe and kindred spirits around us. It is the place that inspiration, joy, and intuition come from. Hard times and sorrow can beat us down, cover up our connection with the sacred, dim its light, or silence its wisdom, but it is still there. Apart from any belief system or tradition, there is something ancient and pure to be honored in all of us. There is nothing to achieve in order to tap into that most precious part of ourselves. It is ever-present.

When we think of the word *sacred*, words like *holy, blessed,* and *revered* come to mind. We associate these words with religious acts, saints, and gurus—but not necessarily ourselves. What if we included ourselves in this level of honoring? How different would life feel if you were to share the sacred inside you on a daily basis? What would that look like? What would that feel like?

Honoring the sacred brought me a new awareness. It informs me of what level of energy I can bring to the day. It enables me to act generously when I need to take care of myself. The sacred in my life is my truth. It is not about pushing the circumstances of my life away but rather dealing with what is in front of me with honor and respect. It's about being in a relationship with something greater than what meets the eye or mind. When trouble hits, if we are not paying attention, we can act in ways that are inconsiderate, disrespectful, and harmful to ourselves. This can have a devastating effect on our hearts and spirits and separates us from the sacred in us. Believe in the sacredness of who you are with confidence, power, and humility and it will transform the way you see the world.

LETTING THE SACRED IN

When I brought the sacred into my day-to-day life and held it up against the emotions that hurt me, I knew that I had come home to myself. I wondered how I had gotten so far away from that place in the first place. I understood that it had not always been like this. I did not believe I was born this way. I was born with love inside me, an effortless kind of love that comes from a childlike innocence. It was later that I learned to judge and criticize myself. I had even learned to hate myself. I started asking questions like:

* What situations and emotions pulled me from honoring myself in this way?

* Why didn't I feel deserving of love and honor?

* How could I change my life to bring back nurturing self-love?

* How could I tap into that fantastic feeling of purpose, a connection to something bigger than myself?

Opening myself to the idea that I was sacred was both compelling and intimidating. It became easier when I realized how simple it was for me to see the sacred in others. My teachers, my mentors, my friends, my loved ones—I could clearly see and feel the beautiful light within them. It was the easiest thing in the world for me to love and honor them. The people who inspired me the most had self-confidence, not in a selfish way, but in a way that raised the bar of how they lived their lives. They tended to their lives in a way that honored their energy, their hearts, and their passion. When I turned the tables and asked if I was ready to bring that same level of reverence to myself, it seemed foolish not to.

Do you know people who embody the sacred for you in this way? If so, learn from them. They will be your mentors, people who will guide you as you travel home to yourself. Likewise, when we see ourselves as sacred, we offer others the chance to see the sacred in themselves and the whole community is elevated. We offer our generous hearts out to those who don't yet have the strength to see the sacred in themselves.

Close your eyes, wherever you are right now, and say out loud: "I am sacred, I am sacred, I am sacred." Each time you recite those words, you get a big dose of self-love. Let me guide you back to that place inside you that is sacred. Let's lift the veil that separates you from your sacredness and tap into the part of you that already knows this to be true.

YOUR SACRED SPACE AND DAILY RITUALS

Every wellness activity requires tools. My yoga mat, yoga clothes, blocks, and other equipment increase the effectiveness of my yoga practice. You need good sneakers for running and a sturdy bike for cycling. Likewise, meditation requires sacred space. It is the place we create to meditate, and through consistent practice, a place we bring our energy, each day, to be felt and processed. The more we go to that place in stillness and reflection, the more power the space holds for us and the more we depend on the space to embrace us.

When you bring your energy to your sacred space, you take a seat with yourself and your highest source. You honor the importance of making time to be with your life. You have created a space that is comfortable and private, and it draws you to it because you have adorned it with things you love. This in itself is an important meditation. You have taken time to create a place that holds you, and before you do any sort of formal meditation practice, you sit or lie there and breathe. Think of this physical place as your temple, a place you take your heart to feel safe, and a place that you can always go to when life feels challenging.

Having a permanent space may not be possible for all of us, but with intention we can create a sacred space anywhere. To make my practice portable, I use a yoga bag to hold everything I have in my space: my sheepskin, timer, journal, mala beads, tissues, and pictures of loved ones. It is intention that matters most; if you have to relocate your meditation space every day or pick it up because the space is used by others too, that is perfectly fine. This is your creation; trust that you will know exactly how to make your sacred space ideal for your needs inside and outside.

Rituals are a sacred part of our lives as well. Rituals can be as simple as your daily run to the coffee shop where you visit with people in your community or the walk you go on with your dog each morning. Rituals are the practices in our life that are important enough for us to make time for no matter what. When we make time for the things we love, we are practicing self-love and honoring the sacred in ourselves. We recognize that we are worth the time and energy spent, and it makes us feel good. What do you make time for in your life? Most likely you already have rituals alive in your life whether you're aware of it or not. Identify and build on them.

MY SACRED SPACE

As a novice meditator, the physical space I created to meditate was my reminder of the sacred in me. It was a physical tool that guided me back to myself each day. The energy of the space drew me toward what I loved most about my life and brought light to roadblocks that stood in the way of my happiness. My sacred space illuminated my intention to come home to myself. I understood that this was not just any room or area; this was a place I was bringing my prayers, and this was a place that would cradle my spirit.

I put pictures of loved ones still on this earth as well as those who were gone in my sacred space. I had pillows and a stool nearby to provide comfort. I picked a light wool throw to cover me when I was in *savasana* (relaxation) and I had a box of tissues nearby to soothe my tears when difficult emotions appeared. I had a timer to help me keep track of time and a journal nearby to write down my feelings.

As I spent more time in this space, I would add meaningful items to it and take out things that no longer served me.

I kept my sheepskin clean and the pillows and other items around my space tidy and dusted. Over time I came to relate to the space far more from an internal perspective than an external one, and the reverence for this physical space began to spill over to other parts of my life. I then began to feel drawn to creating sacred space, little altars, not only in my meditation area but in my kitchen, bathroom, on my deck, and in my garden. Outdoors I'd create an area with a fountain, rocks, shells, and statues, and indoors pictures, candles, and trinkets that held meaning or inspiration. Sometimes it was just a photo in the corner of my bulletin board or a spiritual pendant that hung from my rearview mirror, something that reminded me, each time I would see it, of the intention I had when I created it, and just this observation would snap me back to the present moment and encourage me not to get carried away by worrisome thoughts.

Altars are a way for us to bring physical meaning to our hopes, dreams, and fears. They allow us to take the events of our lives and offer them a chance to be heard and seen through a material offering. Altars are sacred spaces and a wonderful way to bring consciousness to matters of the heart.

There are no rules for the creation of altars or sacred spaces in your life. Just think of it as a practice of creative expression that pays tribute to your unique inner self.

PRACTICE: CREATE YOUR SACRED SPACE

1 **Pick a spot that's private and won't get disturbed.** Ideally this is a corner that belongs to you alone. Give thought to how much room you'll need to stretch out your body, especially if you are going to do yoga or other exercises in the space. Your spot should have gentle light. Consider the direction that your space faces and the view. Seek a space that is as quiet as possible. Above all, it should be welcoming for you. The more you come to that special place, the more familiar you will be with it and the more you will be energetically called back to it.

2 **Make your area comfortable.** Dust and wipe down the surfaces to give your space a feeling of freshness. You can energetically clean the space by setting down a bowl of salt water to absorb and transform negativity or other disturbances, or you can burn sage or incense, or do both. The most important part of your sacred space is a comfortable place to sit so your body can feel settled and quiet and the agitation of your mind is soothed. In Kundalini yoga, we use a sheepskin, but a folded natural fiber blanket will also work beautifully. Feel free to use a meditation stool, a chair, or stacks of pillows. You decide what suits you best. Remember that you are the one steering the ship, so it's up to you to figure out what best suits you.

3 **Adorn your space.** Add a shelf or small table and make a display of things that hold meaning for you: photographs, artwork, prayer cards, jewelry, candles, incense, natural objects, books, and so on. Some people like to bring a "treasure box," a small, ornate container filled with meaningful objects, to their sacred space. Whatever you do to adorn your space, do it with intention and awareness.

4 **Bring your journal and a pen.** So much thoughtful work will take place here that you might want to make notes in your journal. A box of tissues may also be useful, as may a meditation timer or small clock.

5 **For those of you on the go, condense the essentials** to their
   most portable form. Take your mat and blanket or sheepskin with
   you in a tote. Find a special pouch to carry your sacred items in.
   Bring a sense of continuity and familiarity to your experience
   by stimulating your senses the same way every time, no matter
   where you are: feel the same blanket under you, smell the same
   incense or oil, hear the same timekeeper, and see the same
   candles or cards.

You are building your practice from the bottom up. Your sacred space
will help you remember and honor the commitment you have made to
yourself. This space is your temple, your place of worship. Be mindful
and generous in creating it.

PEELING BACK THE ONION

To build a new foundation for our lives, we have to go inside to see which
feelings and emotions are showing up to be healed. The sensations that
scream loudest are the very ones that call us to them first and oftentimes
can be the scariest to deal with. They affect our lives in the most
profound ways, and our tendency—a natural one—is to run from them
because they hurt so much! They tighten and restrict our muscles, they
fog our minds, and they induce anxiety and distress. It seems almost
counterintuitive to want to turn toward them, but that is what it takes to
heal through them. We have to peel back these painful events and learn
healthy ways of addressing them so they can be soothed.

   Like peeling back an onion, layer by layer we look at what appears.
If this feels scary, don't run for the hills; stay steady and know that you
are beginning to cultivate the strength to look inside yourself. Opening
the door to the sacred within, creating a safe spot with the sacred space,
and the other healing practices in this book will put you in touch with
yourself in a way that will surprise you. You can be assured that anytime
you undertake a spiritual journey of healing and ask for the universe to
support your growth and healing, you will not be given more than you
can handle. So stay the course, take your practices seriously, and keep up!

PART
TWO

CONNECTING THE FOUR ELEMENTS OF HUMAN LIFE:

BODY, MIND, HEART, AND SPIRIT

The guiding concept of this book is what I call the Four Elements of Human Life, the physical, mental, emotional, and spiritual parts of a person. They are deeply interconnected, and all four of them must be healed for us to live the most balanced and happy lives possible. It's a theory of knowledge that I have developed over the course of decades with its roots in Machaelle Small Wright's *Perelandra* methodology, which celebrates the power of the individual.

The body, mind, heart, and spirit each have their own unique needs. Our daily habits nurture or inhibit the growth of each of these elements together and on their own. Some elements can grow very strong while others get weak. The body can be injured or get sick. The mind can be distracted or negative in its thoughts. The heart can be overwhelmed with sadness or anger. The spirit can be dampened or ignored. Every sort of imbalance is the warning sign of a bigger problem, and the whole self cannot be healed until each element is considered, balanced, and revitalized.

In times of extreme stress, how often do you take on a negative attitude or get sick? How often do you feel challenged in your relationships by a short temper or unkind words? How often do you feel drained, or even lost, in those extremely stressful times? These are all examples of Four Element imbalances. The body, mind, heart, and spirit call out through pain and suffering, begging you to notice the warning signs and pay attention to the lessons that their pain is trying to teach you. If we are really listening, we start to feel how much this pain affects our lives. But when we are not listening, we miss the messages. Pain hurts the body, distorts the way we think, restricts the way we love others, and invokes fear in the spirit.

Once we understand how valuable each of these elements is to our overall health, we soon begin to pay close attention to the information in those messages. We can identify warning signs of depletion. We no longer have to wait for a full-blown disaster to seek help. It is through this awareness that we recognize what calls out to us to be healed. No matter how distraught you might feel right now, know that you will always have the chance to rebalance and restore the energy of each of the elements and your life as whole.

PRACTICE: MEETING THE FOUR ELEMENTS: BODY, MIND, HEART, AND SPIRIT

The object of this practice is to learn a different way of relating to yourself in which your body, mind, heart, and spirit begin to feel familiar and safe to you. To do so, rather than looking at yourself from the outside in, you'll start to relate to yourself from the inside out. From there you'll bring your attention to each of the Four Elements. You may not be in the habit of thinking deliberately about your body, mind, heart, and spirit, but opening yourself up to this level of self-awareness can be transformative.

Each element will send you information to help you understand how to make your life more comfortable. Begin this practice today and continue every day for the next month. Do your best to do it for the full month; otherwise the changes may not set in. Set the practice to memory, and try to perform it in the same place and at the same time of day. Note that you also can access this practice to help feel grounded during intense situations.

— TO DO THE PRACTICE —

1 Find a quiet, private place, sit down, and get comfortable. Have a piece of paper or a journal and pen available.

2 Take a deep breath in and out. Then inhale awareness, exhale judgment.

3 Say out loud or in your mind (whichever feels more comfortable), "I am open to experiencing myself from the inside out."

4 Take another deep breath. Say the name of the First Element: "Body." Take a deep breath. Repeat a second and third time.

5 Say the name of the Second Element: "Mind." Take a deep breath. Repeat a second and third time.

6 Say the name of the Third Element: "Heart." Take a deep breath. Repeat a second and third time.

7 Say the name of the Fourth Element: "Spirit." Take a deep breath. Repeat a second and third time.

8 Ask your body how it feels. Sit quietly and open yourself up to an answer. Write down anything important that comes to you. Do your best not to judge or reason away any answer that appears. Trust the first feelings that come to you.

9 Repeat by asking your mind how it feels.

10 Repeat again by asking your heart how it feels.

11 Repeat once more by asking your spirit how it feels.

12 Close the practice by thanking the messages that appeared.

PRACTICE: TAKING A PERSONAL INVENTORY

Using the Four Elements of Human Life—the body, mind, heart, and spirit—I will guide you through an evaluation of yourself. We will start with our physical body and then explore the climate of the mind and the condition of the spirit. The more fluent you get in the language of your inner world, the more efficient your self-care knowledge will become. You will gain the opportunity to filter, manage, and responsively deal with situations that have caused pain in the past when you ignored or misunderstood the warning calls of your four elements.

There is always a relationship between the Four Elements of Human Life, and when we can understand the strengths and weaknesses of each, we have the chance to heal potential problems before they arise.

The questions I will ask you next will help you to start a new level of inquiry in your life. What can feel quite mechanical in the beginning will soon, with practice, become a very natural way of addressing the circumstances that appear before you. When I meet with a client for the first time, I have her complete a form very similar to this one. Her answers allow me to access her goals, understand her lifestyle, and gain more insight to her behavior than even she might have herself. From there, I can tailor the practices that will best support her. While this book can't offer that level of personalization, I hope that you will be empowered enough to *know yourself.* When you assess what makes you feel supported, helps you grow, relieves your burdens, and makes life easier, you have achieved success on your healing path. The practices I will recommend in the following chapters are the most universally helpful of all the work that I do. These are the ones that pull everything together and ground your self-care practice so it feels like a welcoming friend in your life. Try them, and then ask yourself what you need to do to maximize the benefits.

Set yourself up in soothing surroundings, dig deep, and trust the journey you are on. Consider the questions not as an assignment but as an opportunity. Take your time to answer them thoughtfully. I highly recommend writing the questions and your answers in your journal, and put a date on the page so in years to come you can look back and witness your growth and healing.

As you are answering the questions, notice when a question evokes a strong feeling in you. If a question makes you happy, why? If it makes you feel hesitant or makes you want skip it, why? This is not an exam, and there are no right or wrong answers. It's simply a chance to get to collect information to understand your goals and recognize the roadblocks to your goals.

Stop when you need to stop and be dedicated to returning when you feel you can. Take as much time as you need; there is no need to rush. My hope is that these questions will illuminate parts of your life that have existed in the shadows and have been longing to come forward. Now is your chance! Lift the curtain and shine light on your whole being. Be patient and considerate of yourself and you will find the compassion you need to continue on. You have come to this book for a reason. Be an adventurer in your life, and stay steady as you move ahead.

Body

1 How would you describe your body?

2 In describing your body, what sorts of words were you drawn to use? Which qualities or body parts did you focus on? Beauty standards, physical stamina, past experiences, your feelings about your body, something else? Why do you think you chose the words that you did?

3 What sorts of circumstances make you feel at home in your body?

4 When have you felt especially strong or powerful in your body?

Mind

1 Is your mind a friendly place for you to be?

2 What do you value the most about the way your mind works?

3 Do you lead your thoughts, or do your thoughts lead you?

4 What makes you feel curious?

5 What topics are you an expert on?

Heart

1 Are you an emotional person?

2 How would you describe your relationship to your heart?

3 Is it easy for you to name your emotions as you feel them?

4 Do you trust your heart?

5 When does your heart feel the safest?

6 Are you able to take steps to manage your emotions when you get overwhelmed?

Spirit

1 Does spirituality have a role in your life? What is it?

2 What makes you feel connected to something bigger than yourself?

3 When does your spirit feel most alive?

4 Are you open to expanding your life, making it into something bigger?

chapter **8**

The Body

Of the Four Elements, the body is our most solid foundation. With a
healthy body, great strides of healing can be made in the heart, mind,
and spirit. Creating a self-care regimen begins with the body. Each of
you will have a different relationship with your body. Some of you may
be similar to me: a natural athlete when I was younger who stopped
listening to the warning signs of an overstressed lifestyle until illness
and injury literally stopped me in my tracks. Some of you might have a
complicated relationship with your body, too used to having your body
judged by society's harsh and unrealistic standards. Some of you might
be survivors of experiences that took a toll on your body, carrying
physical scars in addition to emotional, mental, and spiritual scars.
Some of you might know your bodies as powerful machines, capable of
healing, growing, and even bringing new life into the world.

Listening, learning, and honoring the body's messages is a beautiful
way of opening up to all sorts of healing opportunities. When we
go inside and consider what the body is trying to tell us, a world of
knowledge is revealed to us. Discovering how the health of the body is
woven into the well-being of the heart, mind, and spirit is life-changing.

Your body is the temple of your life, the sacred place where you live.
When we honor the body, the body speaks to us constantly. We are able to

assess how stress affects us and do something about it sooner rather than later. We know when we are tired and need to rest and refuel. We don't need to wait until we catch the flu, get foggy from lack of sleep, or feel overcome with anxiety or depression. Creating a deep awareness of the body clues us into the telltale signs of depletion before major problems interrupt daily life. As we learn to listen to the sacred information that the body urges us to hear, we can respond lovingly with gentle self-care.

The body is a bold messenger. It holds nothing back. It delivers hammering headaches when life becomes too stressful, gives neck pain and a sore throat when we can't express what's really hurting our heart, and brings on an upset stomach when we have been clobbered by something hurtful. The body is what catches our attention first and has us reaching for ways to try to fix it. Through pain, its messages are pushed in our face until we take steps to heal.

Getting in tune with your body means understanding the relationship between what's going on inside your body and around it. One very obvious manifestation is chronic pain, which can flare up when the body is weakened by other circumstances. Awareness opens the door to prevention and healing. I want you to notice discomfort as it comes on and work to soothe it, then try to understand what triggered it in the first place. We grow from pain when we choose to face it, not run away from it. When you identify the areas in your body that bear the burden of your life, you can detect how energy flow becomes restricted in those places and how the heart, mind, and spirit are affected as well. This type of inquiry will allow you to have a deeper knowledge of yourself. You won't depend on others to fill you in on how you look, how you feel, and how you should manage your time and energy. You will already know!

In my life, yoga, meditation and breathing exercises, and time spent in nature are essential self-care practices. They connect me with the inside information of my life and allow me to listen to my body's needs. From there I can act compassionately with what shows up. The messages that arise give me important information on how to work with my body;

instead of feeling aggravated by physical discomfort, I feel grateful for its messages and am able assess what action needs to be taken.

THE BODY IS LIFE'S VEHICLE

The body carries us through life. Without this means of transportation, we have little ability to make much happen. Let that simple knowledge inspire you to take ultimate care of your precious vehicle.

In my own life, I never fail to be astounded by how resilient the body is, even when I am not paying attention. It breathes for me, beats my heart, and moves blood and toxins to help me live optimally. The body does so much for us without us being aware of it. Imagine what it is capable of doing when we *are* paying attention. How would your body feel if you ate nourishing whole foods, exercised daily, alleviated every moment of stress with self-care techniques, and cultivated a way of life that had laughter, purpose, and meaning in it? What would be different? What would your life look like?

There are many healthy choices you can make for your body, and you already know what many of them are: lots of exercise, a balanced diet full of organic produce, and rejuvenating sleep habits for starters. There are two more that I consider essential: healing breath and yoga.

LEARNING TO BREATHE TO HEAL THE BODY

In a world where so much illness is a product of stress, learning how to neutralize stress through the breath becomes a sacred tool for healing. Breathing is one of the most effective tools we have to calm the nervous system, lower blood pressure, decrease heart rate, and soothe the mind. After you become accomplished at breathing practices, you will wonder how you ever lived without them.

Breathing is a great indicator of health. In moments of tension, we tend to choke ourselves of breath, gasping when we're alarmed. Because of our inability to balance our big, busy lives with rest and healing, we tend to go to the sympathetic nervous system's fight, flight, or freeze response, the body's instinctual way of getting us out of danger when threat appears. In this state of threat, the breath is shallow, sometimes inaudible, and feels separate from the body. The trouble is, our sympathetic nervous system can go into this mode as a result of regular, everyday stress—not just when a predator appears. This is a challenging way to live, one that contributes to rapid aging and deterioration of organs, muscles, and tissues.

The great news is that there is a solution, one we can access easily if we are willing to learn. When we take a shallow breath, the breath only moves to the upper thoracic, the collarbone, which has limited benefits for our overall system. It is in this state of shallow breathing that we feel the breath as a burden instead of as a valuable healing tool. When we are separate from who we really are and therefore the sacred in ourselves, we get frustrated by our breath's attempts at waking us up. When prompted to take a deep breath, some people incorrectly have the instinct to clench their bellies during the inhale, constricting the lungs and leaving no place for the air to go. Let's learn how to take a healing yogic breath instead!

THE HEALING BREATH

My whole perspective changed the day I joined a yoga class and learned that there were healthy and unhealthy ways to breathe. Who knew you could breathe incorrectly? Among the body's involuntary functions, breathing is one that can be done inefficiently. While the body is receiving the oxygen it needs to survive, it's often the case that it's not getting what it needs to *thrive*. After learning how to breathe in the most efficient, healing way, the yogic way, I was astonished at how powerful a healer the breath could be. Until you apply yogic breathing techniques to your life, there is no way of describing their potency. The effects of yogic breath have enormous benefits to our physical being, heart, mind, and spirit.

To take a yogic breath means inhaling and expanding the abdomen, allowing the diaphragmatic muscle to drop down and grab the oxygen. On the inhale, the belly stretches away from the spine. On the exhale, the belly releases and moves toward the spine, letting go of stale air and toxins. Like any unused muscle group, the deep-breathing muscles must be strenghtened slowly. The breathing exercises in this chapter provide the perfect training sequence for healthy, efficient breathing patterns over time.

The healing breath benefits the body in many ways:

* It helps to stabilize and ground you in stressful situations.
* It restores a sense of overall calm and clarity when anxiety is present.
* It rebalances the vitality of the body.
* It lowers blood pressure, cleans the blood, and aids the body in working more efficiently.
* It breaks unwanted behavioral habits.
* It helps to nurture an inner relationship with ourselves.
* It trains the brain not to overreact.
* It helps cultivate intuition, grow inner knowledge, and gain wisdom.
* It calms all of the senses.
* It facilitates compassion and forgiveness.

Just as fear interrupts our lives, it also affects our breathing. There is an intrinsic relationship between our breath and our spirit. If I am paying attention to my breath I have the chance to address what fear does to my breath whenever something happens to disturb me. When I'm not paying good attention, I suck in my breath, sometimes holding it in, and then return to shallow, short breathing. But if I am breathing consciously with a yogic breath, life feels safer, happier, and more accessible.

Put your hands on your belly and see if your belly lifts at all. Don't be startled if it doesn't. Once you bring awareness to your breath, you can retrain it. The diaphragm, the muscle responsible for helping you breathe, can be strengthened just like any other muscle. All you have to do is exercise it and before long you will be experiencing the numerous benefits that yogic breathing can bring to your life.

THE LONG DEEP BREATH

The Long Deep Breath is one of the most ancient, basic, and powerful yogic practices. As it nourishes and heals the body, its many benefits include stimulating brain activity, neutralizing the fear response, rejuvenating the circulatory system, and regulating the pulse. The mastery of this breath can be a lifeline in all kinds of situations.

One of the greatest benefits of developing a strong, restorative breath is the feeling of expansiveness that it brings to our life. The depth of our breath is a good indicator of how we live overall. Shallow breathing patterns only allow us to access the superficial aspects of life, and we are merely breathing to survive. The activation of deeper breath allows us to shift our energy and affect healing in our body, mind, and spirit.

The Long Deep Breath could also be called the life breath, because once you've learned and experienced it, you can use it every day for the rest of your life. It will inform you about levels of discomfort in your body, tell you when stress and anxiety are present, and give you deep appreciation for how you feel in any given moment. Breath is the voice of the spirit and your guide, and the more expansive and accessible it is, the more you will tap into primal information about yourself.

The Long Deep Breath is the foundational breath for all breath work. It can be done as a practice unto itself, or you can build on it to work with other breathing techniques. It can activate and invigorate your system, and it can be used as an effective tool for balancing, restoring, and calming. Think of the Long Deep Breath as a healing friend that reveals all sorts of information about your inner world. It will help you understand the nuances of your life, what makes you feel safest and what makes you most frightened, and then give you guidance on how to deal with what arises.

You will feel physiological and psychological benefits immediately after practicing this breathing technique. With it you'll transform difficulty into learning opportunities. Your whole being will pause, giving you time to adjust to new circumstances rather than pushing them away. Your heart rate will slow down, your blood pressure will lower, and you will have the ability to cope with whatever is going on at the present moment. In moments of stress as well as in calm moments of reflection, the Long Deep Breath will bring a sense of expansiveness into your life and offer you a connection to the deep resources inside.

BODY PRACTICE #1:
THE LONG DEEP BREATH

This simple practice will give you knowledge about how you are breathing and help you understand the subtleties of breath. As you become familiar with this breathing technique, you will have the chance to use it in the many situations and circumstances of your life. If thoughts of judgment pop into your mind, notice their arrival and do your best to release them by bringing your focus back to the breath again and again.

— TO DO THE PRACTICE —

1 Sit in a chair or on the ground in a position that allows your spine the ability to lengthen. Use whatever pillows or props you need to make this position as comfortable as possible.

2 Sit tall and feel the crown of your head reaching toward the sky.

3 Tip your chin just enough to lengthen the back of your neck, so your breath can flow freely.

4 Place your hands on your belly and breathe as you normally breathe. Notice: Is your belly pulling in when you take a breath, or is it pushing out? If your belly pulls in on the inhale, your breath will be shallow, with the air entering only the upper part of your lungs. When your belly expands with the inhale, your lungs inflate like a balloon and are filled with fresh air. This is the correct way to practice the Long Deep Breath.

5 Keep your hands on your belly as you practice. Inhale. Feel your chest lift and your belly and ribs expand. If your breath doesn't make it to your belly at first, don't worry. Allow it to go where it feels most natural, and over the course of time, work toward moving it deeper and deeper into your body. With practice and dedication, it will happen.

6 Exhale. Feel your belly and ribs release and deflate, first from your belly and up to your chest. Let all the air from your lungs go.

7 Start again.

8 Repeat the breath for three minutes.

Do this simple practice once a day for forty days to reap its life-altering benefits. You can also bring the Long Deep Breath into any situation either sitting or standing even for a few seconds or a minute when an element of calming and equanimity is called for.

BODY PRACTICE #2:
ALTERNATE NOSTRIL BREATHING

Alternate Nostril Breathing brings awareness to the flow of air that moves through each of our nostrils at any given time. This may seem insignificant, but it actually is very important. Breathing through each nostril brings a different benefit. The left nostril encourages relaxation and calm, the right nostril energizes our overall system, and alternate nostril breathing is helpful in balancing the two hemispheres of the brain, improving sleep, bringing on clarity of thinking, and returning overall balance to the body. Alternate nostril breathing is a beautiful preparation for meditation.

Here are some other benefits of this potent breath:

* Calms the nervous system
* Regulates the cooling and warming systems of the body
* Quickly energizes the body, mind, heart, and spirit
* Helps counter insomnia
* Brings awareness to feelings and emotions in the present moment

1 Sit cross-legged or in a chair or stand in a comfortable position.

2 Relax your left arm and rest your left hand in your lap with the palm facing up.

3 Lift your right arm and press your right thumb against your right nostril. Your right nostril should be closed off but not in a way that's uncomfortable.

4 Inhale slowly through your left nostril.

5 When the inhale is complete, close off your left nostril with your pointer finger and exhale through your right nostril.

6 Inhale through your right nostril, change finger position, and exhale through your left nostril.

7 Repeat the motions above for three to six minutes of breathing.

8 Close the practice by releasing both nostrils and taking a deep breath in. Hold the breath for a count of ten, then exhale slowly.

BODY PRACTICE #3:
BREATH OF FIRE

Breath of Fire is an activator of power in the body that strengthens the navel center, the part of our energetic system where power is initiated. It is particularly useful when your energy is low and you need a boost. Think of fireplace bellows and how much air they supply to make the fire roar. This is what the Breath of Fire does for the many systems of the body. Because of its potency, Breath of Fire is not right for every person or every situation. When we don't have a true understanding of the powerful healing capabilities of the breath, it can be easy to overlook its potency.

Avoid the Breath of Fire if any of the following apply to you:

* You are menstruating or pregnant
* You have experienced vertigo or dizziness of any sort
* You have shortness of breath
* You suffer from heart palpitations
* You suffer from seizures or epilepsy
* You suffer from high blood pressure
* You suffer from gastric issues of any sort

Breath of Fire is a stimulating breath that is practiced in Kundalini and other yoga traditions. It is used to activate and detoxify the body and supports healing and revitalization of the body. In the short term, Breath of Fire will help you feel the connection of breath to body through the respiratory and cardiovascular systems. It will aid you in understanding where there is depletion and where there are imbalances. It will give you a starting point for healing. In the long term, it will strengthen your core and increase your body's vitality, helping to heal imbalances and bring even more awareness to your breathing patterns.

— TO DO THE PRACTICE —

1 Sit on the floor or on a chair. If you are on the floor, try to get your legs in a cross-legged position. If this is uncomfortable, place pillows under your tailbone to support the position.

2 Close your eyes.

3 Take a deep breath in through your nose, stretching your belly as you inhale, as with the Long Deep Breath (page 129).

4 When your lungs are completely expanded, exhale and let your belly relax toward the spine.

5 Fill your lungs again, but this time, with your mouth open, begin panting like a dog.

6 Continue panting, focusing on the exhale to start.

7 When you feel comfortable bringing focus to the exhale, close your mouth and begin doing the breath through the nose. You'll find the inhale will follow naturally.

8 Increase the pace of your breathing with even more powerful exhales if possible. The muscles of your core and diaphragm will be doing all the work. Think of your lungs functioning like bellows for a furnace. Don't be afraid of being noisy! This is a wildly active breathing exercise.

9 Keep going faster until you achieve a natural, even rhythm.

10 Stop when you have completed one minute.

11 Conclude with six slow, deep breaths, lengthening your spine and contracting and lifting your core muscles on the exhale.

HOW YOGA BECAME A MESSENGER FOR HEALING

"Yoga has never been truly described for what it is. It is an art and a science with which you can leap over the pitfalls of life. It is a science and knowledge and art where mind and body can work in union and spirit will back it up." This quote from Yogi Bhajan, the master teacher of Kundalini yoga, the yoga that I practice, captures the important gift that yoga gave back to me: unity in myself. This special combination of movement and mindfulness is thousands of years old. It is the sister discipline to Ayurvedic medicine, two halves of a whole that create a balanced life. Before Yogi Bhajan brought Kundalini yoga to the United States, it was only offered to royalty and governing parties in India. It was known to be so powerful that antiquated governing systems only allowed certain people of wealth and position to benefit from its potency.

Yoga was the messenger for healing my body and, ultimately, my mind, heart, and spirit. Yoga was an opportunity for me to go inside in a way that I had forgotten. Yoga reintroduced me to myself. After years of disconnection, it said, "Remember your body? Remember your breath? Remember your loving mind? Remember your ever-present spirit? And while you're at it, remember that they are all connected to one another."

All these reconnections came alive in me during my first yoga classes. But it wasn't in that romantic, happily-ever-after way. It was more like "Hey, where the heck have you been—welcome back!" Yoga woke up parts of me that had been sleeping for a long time. My early yoga classes weren't soothing, but they were completely enlivening. I was feeling again, not just something but everything. This was such a celebration that even the discomfort no longer registered as pain but as a message and opportunity to heal. It brought my awareness to the restrictions that existed in my body and allowed me to ask "How can I help you heal?" Yes, there were challenges initially, but through modification of the movements and learning how to breathe through the discomfort, I was able to keep up. I found teachers, beautiful beings who appeared like angels in my life at the most perfect time.

Yoga helped me to understand that healing was not about fixing something and then walking away from it. It was about learning a whole new lifestyle and a new way of relating to my body, mind, heart, and spirit in my life. With this knowledge, I would have a direct line to my inner life.

BRINGING YOGA INTO YOUR LIFE

The literal translation of the Sanskrit word *yoga* is "to yoke." This is telling of what the practice accomplishes. Yes, yoga helps strengthen muscles and provides a wonderful cardiovascular workout, but it is so much more. Through slow, careful movement and breath, yoga reveals our inner landscape and our ever-present connection to that part of who we are. As a practice, yoga also reveals information about our life experiences that we have stored in different parts of the body. It is through breath, focus, and movement that we are able to not only access this information but find the strength to look into it as well. This is a deep learning experience, and it takes our healing to another level.

Yoga beckons us home to ourselves. It is a reunion of the senses. Each time we practice yoga, we strengthen ourselves just that much more so we can go inward again and again. Yoga is the companion of a lifetime;

it's a practice that continues until we take our very last breath. Yoga can be as strenuous or as gentle as you desire it to be. It can look like a warrior pose, or it can look like a surrendered child's pose; it can have you lying on your back taking long deep breaths or upside down in a shoulder stand. You decide what would be most supportive to you in that moment. Although awareness of self is what yoga emphasizes, this concept sometimes trips people up: we are so used to the keep-up-with-the-class mentality of workout programs that making the decision to stop and honor where our bodies are in the moment can feel completely foreign. Yoga is not about what the person next to you is doing; in fact, a competitive mind will distract you from the potency of a yoga practice. I think of yoga as my informant. Every day—and every moment for that matter—can bring new information to me. Yoga is my opportunity to witness the sensations and emotions that appear, and it helps me stay true to my life, supplying me with the ability to know how to deal with what appears. The energy of others in a class brings vitality to the group, but comparing yourself to others is counterproductive. Yoga is not a competitive venture.

In the following practices, you'll learn how to incorporate basic yoga poses into your daily life. From there, you may consider seeking out a teacher and joining a class. One of the most joyful benefits of yoga is discovering a new community.

There are many components to a yoga practice, and indeed many branches to this ancient technology, all of them worth a look. It's a fascinating study and one to undertake as your interest and curiosity develop through your practice. But for today, I urge you to make it simple. All you need to know right now is that yoga heals, and it is an amazing adjunct to all healing practices. Only you will recognize what shows up to be healed in your life; yoga can be the tool that supports you in finding it.

WARRIOR POSE

SURRENDERED CHILD'S POSE

Breath and movement are married through a yoga practice; this is universal throughout the branches of yoga. Yogis commit to training their breath so that they can experience *asana* (aa-sa-na), a related group of exercises, in a way that informs them about their experience in that moment. Yogis count on their breath to guide them through a practice. The way they breathe reflects the needs of the body in that moment. If the breath is shallow and fragile, the movement is going to be the same. If the breath is deep and robust, then the opportunity to dive deeper into the pose is available to them.

Bring yoga home to your life. Don't wait another moment. The practices shared with you here will help jump-start your relationship with yoga. They will help you build a practice that will give you the ability to make that practice your own. That is the beauty of the yogic lifestyle: a yoga practice helps us untangle the experiences of life so we can be reconnected to what is most important. It's like watching the clouds clear and once again having a view of the horizon. Yoga delivers the chance to stretch beyond our comfort zone and grow in numerous ways.

Take a supportive approach to your practice: care for, listen to, and work to heal your body through yoga. Back off from any movement that causes pain. Listen to each body part as you go through the motions, gracefully responding to any that hint at resistance, injury, or discomfort. When your body calls for attention, answer with the greatest care. By opening the many channels of your life through the movement, breath, and vitality that yoga offers, get ready to be present in your life more powerfully than you have ever been before.

I have picked four yoga poses to share with you to start or enhance your daily practice. My recommendation is that you do the starting pose daily and pick one other practice to do with it for a minimum of three minutes. If you are inspired, you can do each one of them for the same amount of time depending on what you have worked up to. Doing yoga before going into meditation helps us address the body's needs first so we have a greater ability to sit without the body complaining. Yoga opens the energy centers of the body and allows the channels that are blocked to be released. This aids in healing at all levels.

BODY PRACTICE #4:
YOGA FOR POSTURE (STARTING POSE)

This is where your yoga on the mat and in your life starts. Whether you are doing a standing or seated practice, it is important to begin with Starting Pose. Starting Pose will energize your yoga, your daily activities, and your personal power in the world. All systems work more efficiently when you have strength in your core, lengthening in your spine, and opening through your heart center. Soon this relaxed yet powerful posture will become natural to you as you move through your day.

— TO DO THE PRACTICE —

1 Come to standing with your feet hip-width apart. Or have a seat, move away from the back of the chair, and put your feet flat on the ground.

2 If you're standing, feel your connection to the ground through your feet. If you're sitting, focus on your sitz bones (the part of the pelvis that takes our weight when we sit).

3 From that base, grow and lengthen your spine.

4 Release your shoulders so you feel them melt down into your back. Feel your heart area expand.

5 Level your chin enough so that it lengthens the back of your neck and feels strong.

6 Feel the crown of your head reach toward the sky.

7 Imagine a point between your eyebrows and bring your attention there, continually bringing it back throughout the practice when it wanders off.

8 Stay in Starting Pose for three minutes or up to six minutes, following the yogic breath as it moves in and out of your body, before you continue with your practice.

STARTING POSE

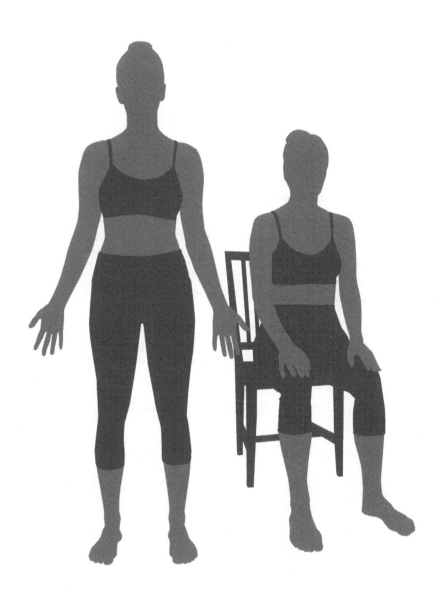

BODY PRACTICE #5:
YOGA FOR OPENING (CAT/COW)

The spine is the first part of the body that collapses when we bear physical and emotional weight. This can happen over time and often isn't recognized until we are in a physical position that puts us in discomfort, with shoulders rounded, pectoral muscles weakened, and the function of our vital organs compromised. We have all seen people who look beaten down by life, hunchbacked and resigned to life's difficulties. In yoga we believe that the spine is the lifeline of the body. When our core is strong and supports our back, we are able to stand up to what we meet each day and stay open to the lessons that come our way. Cat/Cow is a healing practice that keeps the spine strong, open, and flexible.

— TO DO THE PRACTICE —

1 Come into Starting Pose (page 139) and take a few breaths.

2 Come to your hands and knees as if you were going to crawl, with your back forming a tabletop. Place your hands under your shoulders and your knees under your hips and feel the tops of your feet flat on the ground. (If you have knee concerns, work with the modification on the next page.)

3 Take a few breaths and visualize the two animals the exercise is named for: the arched back of the cat and the lengthened sunken spine of the cow.

4 As you move into your cat pose, take a breath and start the movement from the hips. Arch your back in full expression, rounding your neck as though you could touch your belly button with your nose.

5 Exhale and unravel the cat pose, transitioning into cow pose, again initiating the movement from the hips. The spine sinks into a relaxed curve and the chest and upper body come into a beautiful heart-opening posture.

6 Once you have done this a few times, increase your speed and work to make your movements more fluid, really feeling the relationship between the breath and the movement.

7 Repeat for six rounds of cat and cow, or up to three minutes; whatever feels right for your body.

For a modified Cat/Cow:

1 The point of this exercise is to open the back and spine, so practicing it in a chair works really well. Find a seat that allows you to have both of your feet on the ground and plenty of room to flex your spine.

2 Come into a seated starting practice and take a few breaths.

3 Move away from the back of the chair and lengthen your spine with your feet flat on the floor.

4 On the inhale, breathe into your belly and flex your spine forward, keeping your chin as level with the ground as possible. Stretch your belly button as far outward as it will go.

5 On the exhale, release the air from your lungs, draw your belly button back in, and round your back. Again keep the chin as level to the ground as possible.

6 Once you have done this a few times, increase your speed and work to make your movements more fluid, really feeling the relationship between the breath and the movement.

7 Repeat for six rounds of cat and cow, or up to three minutes; whatever feels right for your body.

CAT/COW POSE

BODY PRACTICE #6:
YOGA FOR BALANCE (MARCHING)

This is one of my favorite exercises. It partners breath and movement and has a powerful effect on balancing the energy of the body and the brain. It is fun, and the results can be felt immediately. Just like Alternate Nostril Breathing (page 130), it is useful to turn to when your life feels off balance. There is no need to force yourself through discomfort, because now you have a tool that can help you when things feel shaky. I practice this every morning and throughout the day when I am in need of a reset.

— TO DO THE PRACTICE —

1 Come into Starting Pose (page 139) and take a few breaths. Stand with an awareness of the bottom of your feet on the ground, with your arms by the sides of your body. For a less strenuous option, use the modification on page 145.

2 Lift your right leg to a 90-degree angle and lift your left arm. Stand for a moment in this position, balancing as best you can.

3 Repeat on the other side with opposite leg and arm lifts.

4 Do this twelve times on both sides.

5 Come back to the beginning standing position and take a round of Long Deep Breaths (page 129).

6 Now begin alternating legs. Lift your right leg to a 90-degree angle and touch it with your left palm.

7 Next lift your left knee and touch it with your right palm.

8 After a count of 12, you have completed the practice.

For a modified Marching:

1 Come into Starting Pose (page 139) and take a few breaths.

2 Sit comfortably in a chair. Lengthen your spine, place your feet flat on the floor, and move away from the back of the chair.

3 Follow the same instruction as on page 144, only seated.

MARCHING POSE

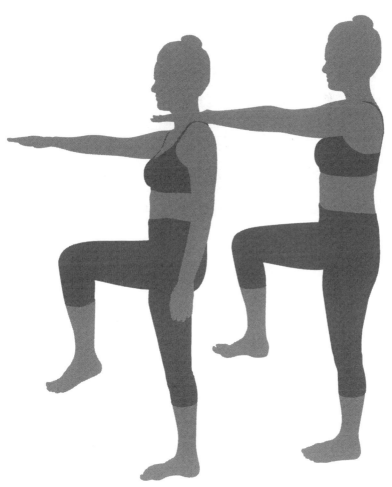

BODY PRACTICE #7:
YOGA FOR CLEANSING (TWISTING)

When we can relate to yoga poses in a practical way, it makes it easier for us to use them as needed. Twisting poses help cleanse the muscles, tissues, and organs and allow a fresh, rejuvenating supply of blood to come in. Just like you can imagine wringing out a towel or washcloth in order to absorb fresh water, that is what happens when we perform twisting poses. The body lets go of waste, and in the process makes room for healing to happen. This is a great practice for the morning to help the body rejuvenate after waking up.

— TO DO THE PRACTICE —

1 Come into Starting Pose (page 139) and take a few breaths.

2 Find a comfortable seat on the ground or on a chair.

3 On the inhale, sit tall with your shoulders square and chin parallel to the floor, and lengthen your spine.

4 On the exhale, twist your hips, chest, shoulders, and head to the right and hold. You will be holding the twist for the next three steps.

5 Take a Long Deep Breath (page 129), and with the inhale, lengthen your spine in the twist position a little more.

6 On the exhale, twist to the right a little more.

7 Take another Long Deep Breath and once more lengthen on the inhale and twist farther on the exhale. Twist as much as you can, but do not push yourself past your comfort level.

8 At your maximum twist, hold for a count of three to six breaths and then come back to center. Check your posture, focus, and breathe for three rounds of breaths.

9 Repeat on the left side. Continue the practice for three minutes.

TWISTING POSE

chapter 9

The Mind

We rely on our mind for clarity. We want to take tender care of our mind, because when it is out of balance it can make life very hard. A mind burdened with responsibility can quickly deplete the vitality of the energetic system. The mind is the initiator of action in life, and it can be one of the greatest allies we have. In order to keep it in good health, we must understand what balance looks like in the mind and, equally, what imbalance looks like. The mind becomes gentler and more efficient when we have tools in place to make adjustments when needed.

To take good care of our minds we turn to our old friend the observer. Notice what your mind is doing right now. Is it present to the information in front of you? Or is it off on another task completely? As you have learned, noticing is a beautiful first healing step and a wonderful way to stimulate the brain and the mind, and it can be a portal to the health, balance, and well-being of the mind.

FINDING THE MIDDLE ROAD OF MINDFULNESS

It is easy to understand how our minds go astray. We process about sixty thousand thoughts a day, possibly more. Some of these thoughts move in and out of us. Grocery lists, random memories, and trivial facts grab our attention for a moment then disappear. Other thoughts stay with us, reappearing over and over again to distract or nag or amuse and encourage. When we aren't able to control our focus, the mind can feel out of control. I think of this as the low road, when the mind is vulnerable to any and all interruptions. An untrained mind runs wild in overreaction, fear, blame, and anxiety. A particularly dangerous habit is to let the mind build storylines, explaining what others are doing with no basis in fact. Relationships can be put in jeopardy when you start believing your own storylines.

Sometimes people go too far in the other direction. Just forcing the mind to stop represses the issue rather than healing through it. Simply rejecting uncomfortable thoughts as they float through the mind is not the answer. It can bottle up feelings and deny you access to a truth that is trying to get your attention. Repressing thoughts lets them live inside you, creating disorder and disease in all Four Elements. Repression calls for too much control and leaves you in constant danger of failure.

Once we have an awareness of the destructive behaviors of the mind, we naturally want to remedy the situation to stop the painful cycle. This is where the comfortable middle road of mindfulness comes in. Mindful self-awareness creates an environment for us to heal. Mindfulness welcomes the lessons that every thought and impulse offers, while also maintaining a firm hold on where the mind's attention goes, like a dutiful parent. There is no need for hyper-control, only a sense of calm and the decision not to judge yourself. With mindfulness we are no longer threatened by the fearful apparitions that loom behind our reactions because we have found a torch to illuminate the scariest of paths.

With a daily commitment to an inward practice, the mind relaxes. It no longer bombards you with a hundred dissatisfactions at once. Mindfulness practice creates a safe space for those dissatisfactions to go. When you notice yourself being wooed by storylines that don't serve you or anyone else, use your mindfulness practice to let them go and heal your mind once and for all.

SHINING LIGHT ON YOUR MIND

Just as the mind is a valuable asset, when it works against us, it no longer serves us and becomes our most challenging opponent. When I was young, I never knew there was a difference between the fair voice of my balanced mind and the critical voice of my ego. I thought that the harsh voice inside me was my conscience keeping me in line, and when it was unkind I naturally assumed that I was deserving of that kind of verbal abuse.

Many of us accept that the mind is less our friend and more our enemy, and this makes for a valid argument why we resist mindfulness. Why would anyone want to spend more time with a voice that continually abuses them? Just like any disorder that has not been healed through, it makes an imprint on the energy of life and continues to hurt us until we find resolution.

Mindfulness exercises help us develop the observer in our lives, so we can sit, witness to the events and circumstances that have harmed us. Likewise, they let us connect even more deeply to that which enlivens us and makes us really happy. Experience yourself in all the elements of your life: body, mind, heart, and spirit. Boldly walk to the places in those elements where there are blocks and restrictions that hold you back from the joy in your life. The guidance I have given you thus far has set you up to do this. We have started at the ground level in building a mindfulness practice, with introductory practices including Finding a Safe Place Within (page 58), Long Deep Breath (page 129), Journaling (page 16), Self-Kindness (page 83), Morning Reflection (page 87), and Seeing Life through the Observer Lens (page 95). There is a valuable reason for this measured approach to self-care for the mind: in order to prepare yourself for the many truths of your life, you have to be strong enough to witness them, hold them, and heal through them. This is a fact. There is no way we can take on hard lessons when we are depleted, worn down, or sick. We have to build up our strength to find freedom from the trauma that has imprisoned us. Self-care is the force that says,

"I am here for you, and no matter what happens, we will find a way home to safety and security."

MAKING MEDITATION WORK FOR YOU

In the daily ritual of meditation, we listen deeply to what our observations reveal to us. We slow everything down by dropping into a space and time that is devoted just to us. For right now, just imagine how sweet it is to spend time with someone you love and how wonderful it feels to have the time to listen to their feelings. How about if that loved one was you? You are worth this time. You are worth this effort. You are worth having a life that feels safe. Meditation can help you create this. This is a chance to quiet the noise of the outside world, spend time looking inward, and build an energetic foundation that holds whatever your life experience reveals.

With self-care practices in place, life becomes an active meditation. When we make self-care practices our number one consideration, we bring a different type of energy to how we live. Very simply, we start paying extraordinary attention, and through meditation, we are able to know ourselves really well. We learn what makes us happy and sad and everything in between.

Through meditation we train the mind and cultivate an intimate relationship with the body, mind, heart, and spirit and learn to respect and honor ourselves. It could easily be misunderstood that something so solitary and inward would only benefit the practitioner, but because meditation enables us to communicate impeccably, it supports healthy relationships with everyone in our lives.

The word *meditation* might have you envisioning a peaceful way of living, but at the same time, integrating that peace into your life can feel unrealistic and unobtainable. I know that I felt that way in the beginning. I loved the idea of meditation, but making time for it wasn't in my schedule—until I realized what meditation meant to me.

You may feel that meditation is for others, those who live quietly, untouched by the demands of our modern world: ancient yogis, monks, nuns, and others who can devote themselves to this kind of inner connection because of the solitude of their surroundings. But meditation is in fact for everyone, and whether we realize it or not we all meditate on something. The deep calm of meditation, also called flow, can take on many forms beyond a formal sitting practice. It can be felt through walks in nature, prayer, even contemplations of the sun, moon, planets, animals, or anything that stirs love in your heart. The key decision is to start with a practice that has us committing to a designated time each morning. This grows our ability to tap into the flow throughout the day. What is it that you meditate on? Is it of service to your life? Now is the time to connect to the powerful energy of your mind, check in with the observer in your life, and make a decision on how to build and grow your meditation practice.

CLAIMING YOUR POWER THROUGH MEDITATION

Any form of personal reflection can be considered meditation. Taking time in your day to witness and hold the many circumstances of your life is an honor and privilege, though it does not feel that way when hurt, anger, and blame are in the forefront of your mind. The untrained mind occupies a lot of space and energy, and it has an impact on everything else in our lives. When we know how to feel safe in the midst of whatever shows up, we become fortified and supremely capable. We don't give ourselves enough credit for the power that we have to heal ourselves. We yearn for someone else to take that responsibility from us because looking at changing the bad habits that keep us from our power often feels too daunting. We look to those around us to reassure us that we are strong enough, beautiful enough, smart enough, worthy enough.

So much of this is learned behavior. We use society's measuring sticks of wealth, beauty, popularity, and so on, rather than tapping into our own personal resources. We ignore physical sensations of pain and discomfort, disregard long-held sadness and depression, and overlook the importance of laughter, joy, and fellowship as a means of bringing healing balance to our lives. It's the easier option to check in with external sources than to meditate for a few minutes each day and look inside.

One of the biggest obstacles to our personal power is ourselves. Our brains are so programmed to stay away from anything that brings on any amount of pain that the first instinct is to run for the hills anytime we feel the tiniest bit of suffering. Meditation holds up a mirror for us to look through and take responsibility for all that shows up, affording huge opportunities for learning and growing. Then we know we're on the right path to building strength and ownership. Then I am beautiful, even though I have that scar on my face or fifty extra pounds on my body, even though I lied last night, said the wrong thing, or did the wrong thing. I am aware and I am learning.

When I started meditating I no longer got away with anything. Every step I took was a conscious step, and when I tripped up, which, as humans we do, my practice in self-awareness would put the mishap in front of me to consider and reflect upon. This level of ownership can be very uncomfortable, but this also is meditation. It's having the ability to turn and meet the discomfort that shows up in life and finding the strength to do what needs to be done to set your life on the right course again.

We run from our power because we are so incredibly powerful. But without a foundation to guide, build, and utilize this power, life can feel like an out of control wildfire.

There is no more important time than right now to hone in on your discipline and commit to this practice. You have built a tremendously strong foundation. Sooner or later, you will be tested. It's up to you to trust that you are ready, that you are worthy, and that nobody knows you better than you know yourself. Regardless of the noise of the outside world, anything and everything is possible for you. Claim your personal power.

MIND PRACTICE #1:
THE INTRODUCTORY MEDITATION

Many people think that the object of meditation is to clear the mind and erase all thoughts from the mind. This is not so! It is an impossible task to empty the mind, and a brain without activity is a brain that is not alive. Our minds are part of us, and as humans we depend on our minds to live. We do not want our minds to be empty. What we want is the chance to teach our minds to be in service to our dreams and aspirations, to champion our efforts, and support us in doing more of what makes us feel alive and happy in our lives, and this takes practice.

This practice will give you the tools to turn your untrained mind into a mind of service. Be the observer in this practice, not the judge, and you will get a lot out of what you witness. Be gentle in your instruction to bring the mind back as it wanders off time and time again. Soon you will have an understanding of your task at hand, and the thoughtfulness of your meditation practice will stay with you throughout the day.

I recommend doing your practice in the morning at the start of your day. It is the easiest time to get it done and move on with a feeling of accomplishment. As your day begins, interruptions that feel so much more important than meditating can get in the way. Allow the time you need in the morning, even if that means you have to wake up a little earlier. You will be happy you did.

— TO DO THE PRACTICE —

1 Come to your sacred space. Silence all phones and other devices and leave them in another room.

2 If the sensory experience is important to you, arrange the same conditions each time: the sheepskin mat or blanket underneath you, incense in the air, silence or neutral sounds such as moving water, sounds of air, or white noise playing in the background.

3 Set your meditation timer for three minutes.

4 Arrive with intention. This is good advice for any self-care practice but especially important for meditation. Arrive with purpose and release yourself to the moment. The opening of your practice is a beautiful time to connect to your higher self and the divine energy around you. I open all my practices by chanting, "Ong Namo Guru Dev Namo" three times. This is known as the Adi mantra and is part of the Kundalini yoga tradition. It means "I bow to the subtle divine wisdom, I bow to the divine teacher within." However you decide to open your practice, come into starting position with your hands in prayer pose at your heart center and take a deep breath, centering yourself at the point between the brows. Through your breath, feel your connection to your higher self and to the energy that surrounds you. Stay here for six breaths.

5 Close your eyes and direct them to the point between the brows.

6 Once you have established the posture, begin the Long Deep Breath (page 129).

7 Hold your attention on the brow point and guide it back when it drifts away from that focus.

8 Breathe long and deep, and listen to the breath as it moves in and out of your body. Feel the sensations of the breath and hear the oceanic qualities of the sound and the warmth it brings to the back of your throat and chest.

9 Ideas, images, and distractions of all kinds will pop into your mind. When you notice that your attention has wandered, simply let the distraction go and bring your attention back to the brow point and the rhythm and sound of your breath. You may only have to guide your mind back once or twice, or possibly many, many times. Simply notice your focus. Don't judge it; just continually guide it back as you would a young child. Every day will be different. Do your best not to build a story around why it is different; simply allow the tides of your energy to flow in and out. If you need to analyze a situation that comes up more deeply, do this another time, not during your meditation practice.

10 Open your eyes when the timer sounds. At the closing of your practice, feel successful in all your efforts. Wrap your arms around yourself and celebrate your amazing courage.

11 Make notes in your journal of thoughts that came up and whether you want to further address them or simply let them go.

12 Close your practice by putting your hands together in prayer pose at your heart center, then take a deep healing breath and bow to your courage, your love of self, and your commitment to show up. I love reading the poem *Love After Love* by Derek Walcott when my practice is complete. It reminds me of how through my dedication to this practice, I come home again and again to myself!

13 Continue this practice for 40 days in a row. At the 20-day mark, increase your daily practice to six minutes.

PRAYER POSE

TRUSTING THE BREVITY AND
CONSISTENCY OF THE BASIC PRACTICE

The introductory meditation is a three-minute practice. Yes, only 180 seconds per day. Everyone has three minutes to spare. All you have to do is make that much time in your life. After all, it is the length of a song or a commercial break. For some of my clients, this comes as a huge relief; for others, I am met with disappointment. They can't imagine how this small amount of time will help them shift from the desperate sadness they feel in that moment. And yet it does! Any amount of time we carve out of our busy lives to hear the callings of our spirit positively reflects back on us. I am suggesting you create a discipline that allows you that opportunity. More does not necessarily mean better, but *always* does mean better. Three minutes is an obtainable goal, one that you can succeed at reaching. The key, though, is to do it! Anyone can do just about anything for three minutes.

When we spend time being in our lives, truly being, we get the chance to witness what appears rather than react to what appears. Meditation encourages this practice of reflection, and the more we do it, the more that feeling of living in the moment permeates everything else we do in life.

Although the practice is short, being consistent about it is what brings lasting changes. In Kundalini yoga, we orient our practices around 40, 90, 120, and 1,000-day commitments. These are sacred numbers in many religions and traditions. All beginners start with 40 days, a sequence that helps to release old patterns and welcome new habits. This period of practice, just under a month and a half, gives beginners the illuminating experience of being on a spiritual journey of self-growth. At 90 days, your new habits will become more familiar to you and you will start to see them influencing the way you act and respond in the world. Fulfilling a 120-day practice will secure these new ways of being in your life. The ultimate challenge, 1,000 days of practice in a row, is a sign of true spiritual transcendence and mastery.

When you have completed this 40-day practice, it is your choice to decide whether to carry on for 90 or even 120 days. For those curious about committing to a 90- or 120-day practice, fulfill the 40 days and ask yourself, "Has the meditation offered me the experience I needed, or is there still more time needed?" Your heart might say yes, or it might say no. If you don't feel complete, keep going to 90 or 120 days. Always reference your instincts and inner wisdom to make this deeply personal decision.

Very often between the 30th and 35th day of a 40-day consecutive meditation practice, a curious thing happens: you forget to practice. You wake up as usual, but for whatever reason, all thoughts of meditating leave your mind and you go about your day without meditating. When this happens (and sooner or later it happens to everyone!), you have to start back at the beginning again. You must start over at day one.

My personal feeling about why this happens is that our minds are attached to our old coping mechanisms. Even if self-care feels better than coping mechanisms, the mind loves routine and is drawn to the most familiar and least challenging way of being. In the initial stages of meditation, the mind doesn't like our insistence that it learn something new. The mind's resistance shows up to sabotage your new path as the ego attempts to pull you from the practice. With this practice, you are leading the ego and mind away from fear and into balance and compassion. While this sounds like a really good idea, until you understand why the mind has attached to the fear in the first place, the ego will continue to throw fear at you. Specifically, the fear that can show up after 30 or 35 days of meditation distracts you from your goal.

Another reason for forgetting to do the practice is that your body, mind, heart, and spirit might need more time to learn before moving on to the next phase of growing. On a physiological level, meditation literally creates new pathways in the brain. For some people, it takes more than 40 days to get a solid foundation for these pathways. In this case, trust the knowledge that comes forth. If you're not ready to let go of this 40-day practice, continue on. You'll know instinctively when you're listening and when it is time to move on to another practice. Pay attention to your experience as you near the end of your commitment, and if you overlook it and have to start again, be grateful for the additional time you will have in this healing practice.

LOOKING FOR DEDICATION, NOT PERFECTION

Let go of the need to be perfect in your practice; simply commit to show up each day and follow the simple instructions. At first the pace is slow, and that is how it is meant to be. This is where cultivating patience is so vitally important. Respect your status as a humble beginner. Remember, you don't run a marathon the first time you go running. There is no race to the finish line in a spiritual practice. There is no competition here. In fact, the very concept of "winning" or "losing" unnecessarily burdens and hinders your progress. The more you can train yourself to step away from the concept of competition, the more freedom you'll have to grow.

When I started meditating, I had a very wise teacher ease my competitive nature by telling me this: "You need to relax into your practice more and just be in it, feel it, and devote yourself to it instead of *doing* it. Really experience what you feel, hear, and sense so you can carry this practice with you for your whole life." That was exactly what I needed to hear, and it shifted my focus. I was given the guidance to slow down rather than treat my practice like another assignment that needed to be accomplished. I came to understand that the most important part of meditation was practicing consistently and making it part of my life, not another item on my daily to-do list.

COMMITTING TO
YOURSELF WITH DISCIPLINE AND DEVOTION

Each morning when you go to your mat, you are making a commitment to yourself. Following through is important. If you don't show up for an appointment with another person, that person no longer trusts you to do what you say you will do. In the same way, when we disregard our agreements with ourselves, we no longer have the trust of our heart and spirit.

Getting to your sacred space and completing your meditation practice is the most valuable thing you can do every day. You need to show up, regardless of bad news, inconvenience, interruptions, boredom, or whatever else life throws at you. Meditation brings discipline and consistency to your brain. It's reprogramming your brain away from fear, anxiety, and anything that inhibits your growth and well-being. There's power in practicing anything with discipline and devotion: the more you do it, the more accomplished and successful you become. You will grow away from that which no longer serves you and toward the things that make your life richer.

Here it is: your commitment to a 40-day consecutive meditation practice. Be invested in your success. I am. Your starting practice will take up no more than three or six minutes a day. This is three or six minutes that will be *your* time for *you* every day for 40 days. This is an obtainable goal. Commit yourself to it, and make it happen. You are worth it!

Please write out these words in your journal as you see them below:

I, [your name], commit to a daily practice of meditation for three to six minutes a day for 40 days, starting [date] and ending [date].

Then, each morning after completing your practice, add this line to your journal:

I, [your name], have fulfilled my promise to myself today. I meditated for three [or six] minutes to bring clarity to my mind and serenity to my life.

TRAINING A STRONGER MIND

When I am out of balance, I am like a cranky child—my body, mind, heart, and spirit keep whining and tugging on me until I bend down and say, "What's going on for you? Is everything all right? Don't worry, we'll figure it out." As soon I have done this, the whining stops and I can get on with my day. When physical discomfort, emotional disorder, heartbreak, or spiritual disconnection show up, these sensations scream at us until we finally bend down and listen. Once we do, miracles happen. This is what meditation facilitates.

You are training your mind through meditation; you have made a commitment to become more self-aware and the ego hierarchy is being altered. The imbalanced ego doesn't like that! Every time you look deeply into your heart and quiet the nagging, fearful thoughts in your mind, you stretch your experience of yourself and become more confident and trusting of your spirit and less reliant on your ego's fearful reactions. Forgetting to do your practice is a message that, for a brief moment, the ego thought it would make another attempt at control. By staying solid in your commitment and starting over, you inform your ego that you are now the captain of the ship and that the fearful information that the mind throws at you is no longer relevant to your decision making.

Remember that every day you go to your mat to meditate, you are getting clearer and making more room for what you really desire in life. Trust the technology of consecutive practice. There is no need to make it harder than it has to be. Taking time to train the mind will make all of your other healing efforts easier and will give you the chance to know life in an entirely different way.

THE FOUR GIFTS OF MEDITATION

Meditation is the portal to a new life. I have no way of telling you just exactly what it will bring to you, but what I can absolutely tell you is that things will shift. Typically people receive four gifts in their lives after taking on a daily commitment to stillness and self-awareness.

The first gift is a foundation for a life that's connected to your spirit and your higher source—the universe, nature, or your God—that will be with you forever.

The second gift is wisdom. Meditation brings us clarity, dedication, deliberate action, and the ability to be guided by inner wisdom. It is a direct line to our power as an individual and to the greater good. Meditation offers us a keen and accurate way of tuning into the mind. Miracles happen in our lives when we begin to investigate our inner world.

The third gift is humanity. Committing to a personal time of quiet reflection every day helps nurture love for yourself and for others. This type of nurturing in your life gives way to all sorts of incredible things. When we meditate, we have access to parts of our humanity that aren't available to us when we move too fast, letting ourselves ignore, deny, and avoid troublesome feelings. When we run away from difficulty instead of moving toward it, life continues to be really hard and gets worse with every new problem. Meditation stops that cycle.

The fourth gift is the ability to learn at a deeper level. Through a stillness practice, what we come to understand is that the difficult situations of life are the most fertile ones for learning. There is a wealth of knowledge in difficulty, suffering, struggle, and fear. Strengthened by meditation, the more settled and safe the mind feels in addressing these lessons, the easier and happier life will become. A daily practice of meditation helps us turn toward difficulty with strength, courage, and curiosity. This connection to higher wisdom is a chance to know life in a simpler, gentler way. Soon we gain trust in the process and go to the practice no longer as a skeptic but as a believer.

RENEWING THE MIND WITH HEALING SLEEP

When we rest the mind, it thanks us by offering us clarity, intuition, and wisdom. The mind is the master control center, processing millions of thoughts a day. While it can perform this function under many less than perfect conditions, amazing things happen when we create comfort for the mind. Because so much runs through the brain, it is always looking for a way to download the information that it receives. In a state of overload, the brain gets tired and performs poorly. That's when we need to take care to rest and renew the brain with healing sleep.

Healing sleep is vital to the health of the mind; likewise, when the mind is overloaded with stressful life situations, it has a hard time running efficiently. It gets overwhelmed with activity. The mind can't heal because it is in overdrive, never really powering down to recuperate. I have seen students in yoga class dealing with this kind of overload: in *savasana,* the final resting pose, they lie down and fall asleep immediately. Some people may think that napping like this is restful, but I see it as the mind's attempt at getting the tiniest bit of healing whenever it can find it. When the body finally stops, the exhausted brain sends the message to go to sleep, right now! Passing out is not the optimal way to rest the mind. Interestingly, sleep does not always come when invited. When we are most desperate for sleep—when we are overstressed and worn out—it can be very hard to fall asleep or stay asleep. A healing sleep ritual is the first thing I offer my clients, because if they are not sleeping well, there is little opportunity for them to address the other difficulties in their lives.

Observe how you rest your mind: are you giving it the chance to rejuvenate, reset, and revitalize? If not, find your healing sleep ritual and make it part of your daily life. Your body, mind, heart, and spirit depend on it!

RESTING POSE

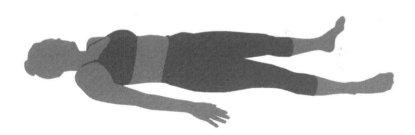

MIND PRACTICE #2:
SINGLE NOSTRIL BREATHING
(RELAXATION/ENERGIZING)

Left Nostril Breathing is a channel for calm, cool, and quiet energy. It restores and heals you and is supportive in relaxing you when your energy has peaked. It also can help when you can't get to sleep or wake up in the middle of the night. Turn on your right side in bed and close off your right nostril with your thumb; make sure your arm is comfortable in this position and breathe through your left nostril.

—TO PRACTICE LEFT NOSTRIL BREATHING —

1 Before you lie down, sit on the side of the bed. Cover your right nostril with your right thumb and breathe through your left nostril for six rounds of breath or longer. Feel the calming effects of this breath and know that with each breath you are telling your central nervous system that it is time to rest.

2 Before you go to sleep, lay your head on the pillow and give thanks for three things.

Right Nostril Breathing is an activating breath and an energizing channel. This is a good breath to do before you get out of bed in the morning. It helps you transition from the drowsiness of slumber into gentle awakening. When you make intentionally smooth transitions from activity to rest or rest to activity, you give the Four Elements of your life the chance to awaken with you and support you where you are in that moment. This breath is also useful midday when exhaustion hits.

1 After you wake up, move into a sitting position on the side of the bed. Cover your left nostril with your left thumb and breathe through your right nostril for six rounds of breath or longer. Feel the energizing effects of this breath, and know with each breath you are telling your central nervous system that it is time to begin activity.

2 Before you stand up, think about three things in your life, big or small, that you are grateful for.

MIND PRACTICE #3:
A BEAUTIFUL PLACE TO REST

Any space created with intentionality is a blessed one. Each time we enter a part of our home that has been adorned with special attention, we tap into a primal sense of who we are and what holds meaning for us.

The bedroom should be our safe haven. A place to rest, rejuvenate, excite, and heal our lives. When we bring this kind of honoring to our space, true healing happens. Take the steps necessary to create a space you love to be in.

— TO CREATE A RESTFUL SPACE —

1 Make sure your bedroom appeals to your senses. I've written a lot about touch, smell, sound, and sight. Bring whatever insight you've learned about your preferences to your bedroom.

2 Decorate your bedroom with colors that soothe you. This isn't the same as choosing your favorite color. Deliberately choose colors that help you feel calm and relaxed. Energizing colors are for other parts of the home.

3 Adorn your bedroom with pictures that make you feel safe and secure and other objects that carry special meaning for you.

4 Be practical as well as creative. Find a mattress that feels blissfully comfortable and linens that are soft and appealing. Make sure your pillows feel good and your blankets offer the kind of warmth and satisfaction needed to sustain long, restful sleep.

5 Make your bed when you wake up each day. Doing so brings finality to the evening's resting period and marks the beginning of the day before you.

MIND PRACTICE #4:
RESTFUL TRANSITIONS

Creating a ritual of rest is one of the best ways to give your mind the message that it is time to let go of the events of the day and shift into another gear. Without such rituals in place to give a clear finish line to the day, we unconsciously float from one activity to another, never giving the mind the okay to let go. When you get home at the end of your day, change your clothes. If you are going to exercise, put those clothes on. If you are staying in to prepare your meal, get into your comfy clothes. No matter what, change out of the clothes that you have worn all day. This is the first step in telling the mind that the concerns of the day are done for now.

1 After you have eaten dinner, start preparing for rest. If you are already in your comfy clothes, brush your teeth and wash your face. If it feels good to you, take a shower, not to bathe but to energetically reset your system to relax and rest.

2 Go to your bedroom and prepare your bed: pull down the covers, fluff up the pillows, get some water for your bedside table.

3 If you watch TV at night, preferably not in your bedroom, make sure that what you watch is funny, light, or reflective. Stay away from the shows that scare you (like most of what is on TV these days).

MIND PRACTICE #5:
AWARENESS IN WAKING UP

Start your day strong and purposefully. This day has so much potential; make the most of how you begin it. The morning hours are energetically charged and have the ability to support us through the day. Lay the foundation for your day through awareness, intention, and reflection.

— TO DO THE PRACTICE —

1 Before you rise out of bed, give your body a stretch. Take a deep breath, and on the exhale, stretch your legs long, point your toes, and bring your arms overhead. Stretch, stretch, stretch.

2 Place your hands on your belly and do five rounds of the Long Deep Breath (page 129; inhale and exhale are one round).

3 Sit up on the side of the bed, and before you place your feet on the floor, take another couple of breaths.

4 If you are feeling particularly sleepy, try the Right Nostril Breath (page 167). This breath is known for its energizing qualities.

5 Take a deep breath that brings in all the light and possibility of the day. On the exhale, release any concerns or worries, trusting that the universe will take care of them in the most perfect way.

6 Start your day!

APPRECIATING THE GIFTS OF A BALANCED MIND

When we learn what it is to be generous, compassionate, and forgiving, offering our support and encouragement rather than our skepticism, dislike, or regret, we have a mind that is working in our favor. When we train the brain to achieve a state of balance, life becomes easier. A well-trained mind knows what to do when difficult situations arise. Troubling thoughts no longer have to be banished into repression or given free rein to further disrupt life. Instead, those difficult thoughts are heard, acknowledged, and weighed in their importance, to be either acted upon or released. Meditation paves the way for your true nature to emerge through your mind. A dedicated practice of stillness breaks down the walls of suffering and allows you more experience with who you really are. We all have the ability to move out of suffering, but it requires discipline and devotion to help us move ahead, and this takes courage. It will take walking to the edge of what is safe and comfortable and moving beyond that to the unknown, that place where it all happens.

Meditation is a practice of getting to know ourselves. In stillness we listen to the callings of our deepest yearnings, our most desperate cries, and our greatest dreams. This can be an inspiring personal experience or it can be terrifying. Sitting quietly and opening your heart is the bravest thing you can do in times of doubt. It is counterintuitive to want to sit when all the alarms go off in your life, but meditation will become your lifeline and deliver you to a place of peace. You may have many guides on this journey, but remember that you are the teacher of your life.

WORKING WITH MANTRAS

Mantras steer your mind in the direction of something positive. Working with mantras is a practice of bringing your mind back into the moment. The beauty of chanting a mantra is that you have no choice but to increase your awareness; you have to pay attention or you'll lose track of where you are.

Protective mantras are helpful at guiding the mind away from fear and toward freedom. When I was first learning about mantras, I wanted to attach to their literal translations, and I often got stuck there. But the mantra practice is more about the vibratory resonance of the words and how that vibration lands in our mind, body, heart, and spirit. When we allow our mantras to resonate through the various aspects of our life, we find a deep level of healing. My teachers encouraged me to chant mantras through my spirit and not get caught in my untrained mind's judgment. In doing this, I soon felt the potency of the practice.

The mantras that follow are from the Kundalini yoga lineage. These mantras have become part of who I am. They are my go-to when life feels fragile. Mantras have given me the chance to change old, fearful ways of being and look toward a hopeful, faith-filled vision of the future.

The *Mangalacharan* mantra is a protective mantra that I have worked with for many years. It goes like this: "Aad Guray Nameh, Jugaad Guray Nameh, Sat Guray Nameh, Siri Guru Dev Nameh." (You can do a quick online video search to pick up the pronunciation.) It roughly translates to: "I bow to the primal Guru, I bow to the truth that has existed throughout the ages, I bow to True Wisdom, I bow to the Great Divine Wisdom."

Even when I didn't understand the translation, I could feel the protective qualities of this mantra embracing me. Chanting it soothed me deeply. To this day I chant it every time I get in the car, think of someone in need, or just feel the need to bring more protective, healing energy to my life. Intention is so powerful, and when you embody intention with purpose, you have a powerhouse of support behind you.

MIND PRACTICE #6:
PROTECTIVE MANTRAS

Find a mantra that resonates with you. Use one you already like or create a new mantra for yourself. Simply choose a few powerful words or phrases that are easy to remember and are packed with meaning for you. Let your personal mantras be your best friend and guide. Start with this simple practice and watch how it grows you in all directions. Here are some other mantras that I use often:

* In this moment, I am safe.
* Slow everything down, now.
* Open, open, open your heart.
* Release the drama, release the fear, and find the truth.
* Breathe long and deep.
* You are safe, you are loved, you are light.
* Find the good in this moment, now.
* I am with you in spirit.

Mentally vibrate or say your mantra out loud when you need extra strength and courage or want to give yourself the chance to break through fear. Make it your go-to response, and from this place of awareness, change will happen.

The Heart

As a young child, I experienced love freely without obstacles. It was a part of what I knew and cherished. Love filled my life. Then everything changed. After the loss of my parents, my relationship to love shifted. Love was no longer something I trusted. Security and love went away. Moving into adulthood, I felt like I needed to protect myself from love, or more specifically, from the threat that it could be taken from me at any time. Love scared me. But what I didn't realize, until much later on, was that I was no longer feeling love: I was experiencing fear.

My mind was drawn to people, places, and things that I loved, but my heart stood back, waiting for the ball to drop, for some loss to happen. It felt like my heart was a bystander, skeptical and detached. I processed through my mind but never actively engaged my heart's energy. I had learned ways of coping with a detachment that looked very much like love, but my behaviors were ruled by fear. I felt like I had one foot in my life and one foot out, poised to jump out at the first signs of love's betrayal. The intense experiences of my youth tangled love and fear up together. Love could mean happiness, but equally it could mean pain. My relationships with my loved ones and my relationship with myself were defined by both love and fear. I stopped distinguishing between the two emotions. Strange as that might sound, until you really understand the difference between the two, it can be easy to blend one into the other. They are both intense, primal emotions, and sometimes only nuances will differentiate love from fear. So it becomes very important that we understand what those nuances are.

FACING VULNERABILITY

When we have been hurt deeply, it is hard to put ourselves in a vulnerable position again, but we have to do just that to find the promise of love again. Taking a look inside to see the sadness of the heart is the only way out of the pain. This is why self-care practices play such an important part in the healing of the heart. Otherwise the pain won't budge because it will feel too big to deal with. It is likely the reason we didn't heal through our trauma the first time: the support systems were not in place for us to do that level of healing. This is not bad or good; it's just the reality of life. The wonderful news is that it can go right this time.

This all might sound simple, like low hanging fruit, too easy to be effective. But don't disregard the power and impact of meditation, yoga, and other self-care practices; soon after you commit to them, you'll know how extraordinarily potent they are. Strengthen your power to look inside and make these changes. Become an astute observer and heal what is longing to be healed in your heart.

TRUSTING THE ENERGY OF THE HEART

The energy of the heart filters through the mind, body, and spirit. This is its great value. When it is activated with awareness, it has the power to bring compassion to our wounds, regrets, and losses and gives us the chance to grow. Likewise, the heart energy flows through those parts already rich with offerings of love.

The energy of love is pure power. The energy of fear is toxic and drains vitality. When we have an obstructed view of love, it is difficult to find hope. Our downtrodden energy can lead to disappointment, doubt, and anger. Trying to find love that's blocked by fear can create more frustration and resistance and lead us into a downward spiral. It's like trying to see a beautiful full moon on a hazy night. It's difficult to find it through the clouds, and you're left wondering if it is there at all.

As energetic beings, our experience of energy can be profound, but when we are blocked from that source we have no experience of its healing potential. When fear overwhelms us, our energy feels restrictive, heavy, and burdensome. There is no room in our physical, emotional, mental, or spiritual selves to deal with one more thing because every ounce of our energy is being used to deal with the symptoms of what fear and pain are bringing up for us. We've all felt the imprisonment of fear in this way. Fear initiates discomfort, anxiety, anger, jealousy, and disorientation, and when you are present to it in your life, you recognize it immediately. Fear is heady, insistent, and disregarding of anything and anybody else but the fear that exists in you. Fear makes us feel small, limited, and continually on guard, ready for the next assault. It rips opportunities for learning, listening, compromise, and forgiveness from us. Fear is the wound that didn't heal, and soon we know that we will spend the rest of our lives protecting and defending that wound. This is fear in all its power. And because there is no energetic room in your life to cope, it invokes tremendous amounts of pain and suffering.

It takes faith to believe that love can live in our hearts when there's no overt evidence of it. The certainty of this presence is achieved over time with a dedicated practice of self-care. There is no faster way to turn personal difficulty around than to ask yourself, "What do I need, in this moment, to feel happier and safer?" Self-care practices bring us back to our lifeline as we cater to the precious heart's basic needs. As our bodies get stronger and our minds get clearer, we address the obstacles that obstruct the energy of the heart, and wounds start to heal.

When we can ask ourselves what the difference between the energy of love and the energy of fear is, our path of self-discovery and healing is accelerated. We turn a corner. We no longer fend off the vulnerability of the heart's longings because we are no longer in the dark about what keeps us from them. We start to remember what it feels like to love without conditions, obstacles, and fear, and we want more of this experience because love feels so good. Love has a way of reappearing when you realize how much you've missed. The walls of fear are broken down and you naturally invite love back in.

FEELING THE EFFECTS OF LOVE ON THE FOUR ELEMENTS

Love ignites faith and hope. Love makes us feel expansive, like everything is possible. This is not just a sweet little sentiment—it is a powerful reality. When we work to nurture our heart's love energy, we heal beyond the fear that exists in life into a place where incredible things can happen. Love's power is palpable. It is inclusive and compassionate and offers us understanding for ourselves and others. Love's power resonates through the Four Elements. When we feel love at a physical level, we open up and clear out the things that hold us down. In our body it can be felt through expansiveness in our chest, lungs, shoulders, and upper back. Love energy settles our minds and draws us to inward practices such as meditation and yoga. Love welcomes us inside ourselves with generous hospitality. It puts us in a higher way of being that unchains us from fear and suffering.

Love's energy heals and fear's energy drains. Being able to acknowledge how your energy feels in your body, mind, and spirit in the moment, you access a major source of wisdom. Tapping into your heart to check whether you are fueled by love or by fear can change your reactions and the decisions you make. Love transforms fear from that monster that wakes us up at night into the diligent teacher who so wants us to be able to move on. When love is present and outweighs fear, space for our thoughts and feelings opens up. Love is the emotion of opportunity, opening doors to what the heart most desires and giving us the chance to believe that it can truly be present in our lives. Love converts fear into stronger love.

HEART PRACTICE #1:
WHAT DOES YOUR HEART SAY?

This practice will ask you to listen deeply to the messages of your heart. The instructions are simple, but don't disregard its value and potency. All of what you have learned up to this point has prepared you for taking this deep look at what your heart has to say. Are you able to identify whether you are feeling the healing benefits of love or are you stuck in restrictions of fear? Do this practice when you're in an upsetting or fearful situation; the objective is for you to notice your emotions and to analyze where the feelings came from, then to let the feelings run their course. When in doubt, ask the question "Am I in fear right now, or am I in faith?" Don't be discouraged if initially you find you are in fear most of the time when you ask the question. You are brave to make the inquiry at all! Your honesty will break through the fear soon enough. This practice requires a lot of concentration and awareness. At first it can feel clumsy and aggravating, but keep at it. Just like anything that you practice, you will get better at it. Before long, it will become second nature to you.

— TO DO THE PRACTICE —

1 Be ready for the cues that call for your heart's attention. These signs can be intense feelings, a racing mind, or physical manifestations like crying, trembling, or an elevated pulse.

2 Excuse yourself. Whatever is happening around you, step away from it. If you are at home, go to your sacred space. If you are on the road, begin a long deep breath, or go somewhere that offers you privacy.

3 Come into your Starting Pose (page 139), either standing or seated. Take a few breaths. Then settle into a comfortable position. If it helps, visit your visualization from the Finding a Safe Place Within practice on page 58.

4 When you're ready, ask yourself this series of questions. Let the answers reveal themselves to you without judgment.

+ What is the name of the emotion I am feeling right now?

+ What circumstances brought on this emotion in me?

+ Why is my reaction so strong?

+ Is my reaction appropriate or an overreaction?

+ Does this situation remind me of something unresolved from my past?

+ What would make me feel safe right now?

+ Are there boundaries I can put in place to avoid this situation in the future or take control of it sooner?

5 Take a few more healing breaths. Return to your day, knowing that you took control and made yourself feel safe. That is a gesture of self-love and a huge step in the right direction.

6 The next time you journal, record this event and the answers that came to you in step four. Also record any reflections you have now that the panic has abated. If you feel the urge to judge yourself, imagine that you're being told this story by your dearest friend— would you respond to her with the same judgments or be more compassionate? Offer yourself this same opportunity.

HEART PRACTICE #2:
SELF-SOOTHING

Over and over again we come around to the question "What does it take to make you feel safe?" Now is the time to get precise about the answer and to fill up your self-care toolbox so you can reach for it in times of stress. These are some general ideas; the important thing is to find the tools that fit like a glove for *you*.

1 Find your temperature. This is a creature comfort that can be easily overlooked, but it is important. Know when your body needs to be warmed up or cooled off. For me, one of the most soothing things I can do is to hold a hot water bottle to my chest before bed. (Mine is heart-shaped!)

2 Find your comfort foods and drinks. There are few things more classically comforting than a cup of warm tea. Food can be a touchy subject, as some of us are drawn to using food as a coping mechanism, but having a shortlist of nourishing whole foods that bring you comfort is a good thing.

3 Gently stimulate your senses. Give your senses somewhere gentle to rest. Choose soft fabrics to feel against your skin. Keep soothing photographs and artwork in the places you spend the most time. Have your favorite music ready on a streaming playlist or try a white noise machine.

4 Nourish your heart with positive entertainment. Our empathy is what makes us unique as a species. Soak up the emotional experiences of others through television shows and movies you connect with. Figure out if you are more soothed by humor, informative entertainment, drama, or something else.

HEART PRACTICE #3:
LOOK IN THE MIRROR

There is no more effective way to get real with yourself than to look into your own eyes and voice an affirmation. It will quickly give you an understanding of your feelings in the moment. If you practice this every day, life will start to shift rapidly as the barriers between you and your message dissolve. Mirror work is the ultimate practice in accountability. When you meet your eyes with the message of forgiveness, love, and acceptance, insecurities melt away.

Sit in front of a mirror at the start of the day, meet your eyes, and name the emotion that is most present today. This is an opportunity to look at yourself, admit the truth of the situation, and congratulate yourself for being honest and in touch with your feelings.

HEART PRACTICE #4:
WRITE A LETTER TO YOUR FUTURE SELF

Take some time in a quiet spot and compose a letter to yourself a year from now. Reflect on the circumstances of your life right now and any small moments of life that you'd like to reminisce about later. Then write down the aspirations you have for the future. How will daily life be different for future you? Which habits, relationships, and emotional cycles will be better? What will you be grateful for and have to celebrate? Give yourself advice and words of encouragement.

When you have finished your letter, seal it in an envelope and tuck it away somewhere safe, like the treasure box in your sacred space (see page 112). Use a calendar app to set an appointment for a year in the future with a reminder of where you put the letter and a time to open it. For a low-tech alternative, entrust the letter to a very organized loved one to drop into the mail a year from now.

BECOMING A WARRIOR OF LOVE

Love and fear do not coexist in the heart. They can't. It is one or the other. I used to think they were two sides of the same coin, and this is what blurred my ability to be a strong and deliberate observer of my life. Fear was full of excuses for careless behavior, disregarding the feelings of others, placing blame, or even its most harmful expression, hate. In fear, a wounded heart is fragile and ready to overprotect the hurt it feels. This is an instinctual response: we shut down when we feel wounded, defending against that which threatens us most. This is a common cycle, and one that I am very familiar with. This cycle of suffering has us falling victim to our lives, adopting habits to protect ourselves instead of healing through the devastating hurts we've experienced. This type of protection holds us back from looking deeper, only allowing us the chance to manage the symptoms, never the origin of the hurt.

When we invite love in, everything shifts. When we take our perspective from victimhood to empowerment, we no longer say, "This happened to me." We say, "Let me look at what I choose to do, how I choose to react. How can I feel more in control? How can I make this right?"

When we recognize the signs of our hurt, we can fully feel the restrictions and suffering it brings us. From there, we have the ability to do something about it. To heal through fear, we have to understand the damage fear does to us. This requires stepping away from numbness and letting fear run its course. It means choosing love over fear, again and again. That's when we start to mend. With the smallest steps in the direction of love of self, we feel stronger and better equipped to let go of what has kept us down for so long.

What you are doing is saying to yourself, "The situation was out of my control. Harm was done to me. Now, I take control and I choose to heal. I do not give permission for any more harm to come from this situation." I am very clear how much courage this takes. This is not something that we all can do right away. It's a huge leap. We have to build a foundation for healing step by step, one that allows each of the Four Elements to rebuild, reset, and rejuvenate. Your pain is real, I am sure. But when does that stop? And will you give yourself the chance to know life in a different way? When will you make the decision to move from fear and feel love?

This loving gesture changes the direction of fear's ingrained path in our lives. What would it feel like to forgive, and what does forgiveness mean really? Does it mean that you have to forget the hurt and pain that has been dumped on you? Does it mean that whoever created the situation was justified in acting out in this way? Absolutely not! But how long do you have to hold on to the sadness it caused? And when is it time to say enough? When will you bring love back into your heart? When we choose to find love in the difficult events of our life, we are also making the choice to find peace. This is an act of high service to ourselves. We boldly state that *no one* has the right to take love from us ever again. We are warriors of love—awake, alive, and living life in full service to ourselves.

HEART PRACTICE #5:
WARRIOR OF LOVE

Sometimes something happens to interrupt a normal day that turns your world upside down. Maybe it was something big, or maybe it was something trivial like a line in an e-mail or the way a phone call ended. Don't deny your feelings. Let this line of questioning reveal more about your healing journey.

It takes great strength to look inside, and this practice asks you to do that and quite a bit more. When something happens to upset you, become a warrior and look deeper than what the outward circumstances dictate. The warrior opens her heart to the big picture, and this opens many doors to healing.

— TO DO THE PRACTICE —

1 Think of a recent situation that made you feel frustrated and not worthy of respect.

2 Feel the emotions and let your fear be exposed to yourself. Feel yourself as the victim of the circumstances.

3 Notice how the victim (fear) feels in your body, mind, heart, and spirit.

4 Come up with a word or description that applies to each of the Four Elements: your body, your mind, your heart, and your spirit. Jot the words down on a piece of paper, in a note on your smartphone, or even an audio recording or voicemail to yourself. Breathe into the feelings that these words bring up and validate the emotions by saying, silently or aloud, "I understand."

5 Now do the opposite. For example, if you are feeling blame, feel compassion. If you are feeling indignant, feel empathy. If you are feeling insistent, feel patient. Look at what might possibly be going on for the other person to have caused them to act out in this way.

6 Now breathe into these feelings and write down how it feels in your body, mind, heart, and spirit.

7 Be gentle and understanding of yourself. If you do not immediately feel a difference, don't rush it. Just bring your awareness to it and eventually things will start to shift.

HEART PRACTICE #6:
TAPPING INTO THE PRESENT MOMENT

You have been using a journal to reflect and grow through the practices in this book. Now it's time to develop an even deeper commitment to the beneficial act of recording your thoughts in a journal. In your daily entries, ask yourself the following questions using the prompts as a means of going inside to tap into the present moment. Doing so will give you the ability to know how to take care of yourself that day. Over time, the exercise will become second nature and you will find yourself applying it to your life often.

— TO DO THE PRACTICE —

Ask yourself:

* How does your body feel?
* How does your heart feel?
* How does your mind feel?
* How does your spirit feel?

Then use the following prompts to spur you on when you get stuck or you want to see how you've grown over time. I wanted to give you many options to pick from, but there is no rush to answer all of the questions. Pick the ones that feel curious to you, the ones that give you the chance to learn more about yourself. Be inquisitive about your answers, don't overthink them, trust your instincts, and write your answers freely.

* What is essential for you in life?
* What does home mean to you?
* What makes you feel safe?
* What makes you feel nourished?
* What makes you feel your strongest?
* When and where do you feel calm?
* What are your favorite forms of creative expression?
* How do you soothe yourself in times of stress?
* What makes you feel productive?
* What is your favorite thing about your private inner self?
* What activity makes you feel passionate, even if you don't get to do it often?
* What sort of reputation do you want in your community?
* How do you feel when you are placed in a leadership position?
* Do you feel in control of your relationship with money?
* When in your life have you felt the strongest sense of personal drive or ambition?
* Do you consider yourself a flexible person? Would others agree?
* What do you like best about the way you treat others?
* What is different about you when you are in love?
* What sort of people bring out the best in you and make you feel proud of yourself?
* If you could forgive something or someone, what or who would it be?
* Are you honest with yourself?
* Are you honest with others?
* What circumstances cause you to rely on dishonesty?
* Can the people in your life count on you?

* What words do you want to share with others, but don't (or can't)?
* In what ways are you an observant person?
* Are you good at making decisions?
* When have you felt wise in your life?
* What sort of patterns do you find yourself repeating over and over in your life?
* In times of stress, are you more likely to reach out in fear or in faith?
* In what ways are you generous, and in what ways could you be more generous?
* Do you trust your instincts? If so, are they right?
* Can you anticipate things before they happen, or do you get gut feelings about things that you can't explain?
* Are you open to and respectful of different opinions?
* In what ways do you feel connected to the world around you?
* What do you believe is sacred?
* When was the last time you felt effortlessly in sync with the wide world?
* What do you do that makes the world a better or gentler place?
* What is your purpose in this life?

RECOGNIZING THE THREATS TO LOVE

Love is at the very root of everything in our lives. It's the driving force. It is the nature of the universe that every force has a counterforce—a certain gravity to keep it in check. A threat to love is a challenge that asks you to recognize an ever deeper sense of awareness. To me the four principal threats to love, be it love of oneself or another, are judgment, jealousy, loneliness, and shame. These threats are all fuel for the ego. How do they present in your life and relationships? What effects have they had on you?

The storied conundrum of the heart is this: love yourself so that you're able to love another. Creating a greater awareness around these four threats to love will allow you to recognize them and keep them in check. When we can go to the heart of difficult, stubborn emotions to face these threats, we become champions of our own lives.

THREAT TO LOVE #1: JUDGMENT

Let's face it: we all form opinions about what goes on around us. It is part of being human. Each one of us has a different lens based on experience, personality, background, and a million other factors. When we are wrapped in fear, overprotective judgment might feel like a friend, a strong defense that moves in to guard us, but in reality that judgment negatively influences how we see others as well as ourselves. But as we move away from fear and toward love, we understand how this has all been an effort to protect our wounded hearts. Judgment is the first line of defense in protecting the heart. Judgment is insidious, infecting everything it touches. This type of protection of the heart never moves us forward. It only exacerbates the hurt we already feel, making us feel even worse.

When we have unresolved hurt, our experience of ourselves is that of a skeptic: quick to doubt, forming very strong beliefs on how we feel about just about everything. In its most broken state, the heart harbors resentment, and that resentment becomes a guiding force. The origin of that hurt affects us negatively until we are ready to address it. The seed of hurt imprints our hearts and grows into more pain and anger. And we fortify our hurt every time we move to protect, rationalize, or blame another for what has happened to us. We go into overdrive to protect ourselves from another threat, and before long have closed ourselves off to our lives entirely.

THREAT TO LOVE #2: JEALOUSY

How many of us have been in the throes of the green monster? Have you noticed what it does to you, how depleted and inferior you feel when you're put up against the object of your jealousy? I realized that in the midst of my panicked responses I had lost all sense of self-worth. The day's actions were being influenced by something that had happened to me long ago, and it blurred my reasoning, my compassion, and my reality.

In a place of jealousy, I disconnected from my heart and stood by a storyline that had no truth to it. I was inviting hurtful beliefs into my heart, and they were tearing me apart. And that was not all: I was blaming someone else for making me feel this way, and often punishing that person for my pain by disconnecting. The wildest thing about jealousy is that sometimes it can be caused unintentionally—the object of envy has no idea she has created this internal storm for you. I had let jealousy inform me that I was no good and no longer worthy of precious love.

Healing through jealousy keeps the chaos and misunderstandings of the outside world from having power over your private, inner self. As we learn to go inside and explore the obstacles that muffle the messages of the heart, we have to find the ability to love ourselves first. We need an understanding of what has the potential to ignite past hurts so we can implement a plan to guide us through that which scares us most. For us to feel positive and healthy, we have to steer ourselves away from a storyline that has the potential to tear our hearts apart.

In a well-established practice of self-care including meditation, journaling, and yoga, it becomes easier to stay focused on what matters and what heals our hearts, and with each step in that direction we get stronger. We trust the heart's intention to keep us safe. Then our external environment—what other people wear, buy, look like, achieve, and so on—dwindles in importance and we can look at other people's success with sincere appreciation rather than envy.

If you look hard enough, you can always find someone with *more*: more luck, more cash, more stuff, more, more, more. But remember: you can't assume to know that person's heart. You cannot know if she is happy or what her relationship to her inner self is. When I was at my most vulnerable, experiencing loss, health scares, and emotional distress, there probably were people who looked at me and thought, "Look at her business, look at her house and her family, she has it all!" What they didn't know was that I was falling apart inside, totally disconnected from the messages of my heart, and that all the outer, successful appearances could not give me what I longed for most, that deep relationship to my heart and spirit.

Our job is to grow a little more every day through our self-love practice. Instead of giving into competitive jealousy, let yourself be humbled and ask, "What can I learn from this?" Listen to your heart and create more connections to love in your life. There is no need for someone else to quantify or qualify our value. Humble self-love waits patiently for us when we wander off, and it welcomes us back with open arms when we return.

THREAT TO LOVE #3: LONELINESS

Among its sources, loneliness can come from loss through death, the natural end of a relationship, or getting left behind. They all hurt. In the long run, though, the hardest loneliness to heal from is the loneliness you feel when you can't fully love yourself. Disconnecting from your heart's energy is the deepest experience of loneliness. We fall into believing we are not worthy of love from others or from ourselves. We take on mechanical ways of being that are rooted in unresolved issues from the past that separate us from self-love.

We struggle through life in this way for a while, but eventually this solitary existence breaks us down. The broken connection to the heart saps us of passion, and life has no spark. Nothing calls to us or inspires us. All other emotions get grayer and more negative. What can you do?

Awareness is a precious tool for healing. Acknowledging the presence of loneliness is the start. From there, we must build our energy back and open up the dialogue with the heart again. Remember the things you love about yourself. When something sparks your interest, explore it. Be aware of what interests you and attracts you to other people and new experiences. Start to grow again. Explore the world in a forgiving way. Gravitate toward anything that feels fun or makes you laugh. When you open your connection to your heart again, you will learn to love yourself once more and start to feel the loneliness dissipate. Then you'll find more room in your life to explore what makes you truly happy. Loneliness came in to be felt and realized, not as a lifelong companion but as an emotion to help you understand that this is not how you have to feel forever. Thank the message it came to deliver, and send it on its way!

THREAT TO LOVE #4: SHAME

Shame is an extreme expression of embarrassment. Embarrassment is hard to get through, but shame raises the stakes so high that it can change the course of people's lives. Shame can be so overwhelming that it is hard for the heart to forgive itself and get over it. Shame pulls the heart away from itself, because shame distorts the heart's energy, making it seem impossible to feel worthy of love. Sometimes shame may be brought on from something others have done, or it may come from something we have done. Shame might come when you're feeling overwhelmed and you lash out, or it might come from a thoughtless action when you were disconnected from your inner self. No matter what the circumstances are, shame is destructive. Mindfulness offers us protection from shame. Whenever awareness is present, we have the ability to catch a situation before it elevates to disaster.

When we become aware of the presence of shame, we have the chance to look at how it got there in the first place. We peel back the outer layers of the onion and view the pain that lives inside the shame. We look at the tender hurt and encourage it to reveal itself to us.

Don't try to reason with shame. Instead, become strong enough to hear what has happened to create the conditions of shame in your life and witness your feelings from a perspective of openness and love. From there, you can work with compassion and forgiveness rather than running from guilt and resistance. All opportunities are open to you from this place!

EMPOWERING THE PROTECTORS OF LOVE

Embracing who we are with all our bumps, scars, and imperfections is the grandest expression of love there is. When there are no conditions required to love ourselves, we love freely and without restrictions. The doors of our life are flushed open and we know life differently than we have before. There are many actions that can get in the way of this free-flowing experience of love. I bring them to your attention not to scare you but so you can recognize them when they are present in your life. That way you can activate your awareness to protect love in your life. As you have heard me say before, awareness is the key to fortifying a healing path. Every action taken in the direction of awareness will secure hopeful possibilities for the future.

PROTECTOR OF LOVE #1: PERFECT IMPERFECTION

When we make friends with our humanity by accepting that we will make mistakes, it becomes so much easier to learn, grow, and train ourselves to feel love even when we trip up. Healing becomes a journey, not a pressure-filled destination. We recognize that there is no more need to feel the devastating boundaries of perfection. Making mistakes is one of the most effective ways of learning, yet we often miss the opportunity because of the distress we feel from not getting it right the first time. In a depleted state, there is a natural urgency to make things right as soon as possible by overcorrecting. We become impatient, and we naturally want to take the fast track to make things wonderful again. The impulse to rush the process is a coping mechanism and a natural response when we are still in a weakened state.

Let this be yet another reminder to go in gently. You are just opening up, and so you will be very susceptible to judgment of yourself. Let go of the need to be perfect in your efforts and instead try to be a diligent learner. When you stumble, brush yourself off and get back up, then celebrate your courage to start again. Feel your shoulders relax, your breath become full and robust, your mind settle, and your spirit rejoice in this celebration of starting over. There is no getting anything right unless it feels right to your heart, so stay steady. When the urge to criticize your amazing efforts shows up, soothe those feelings with the practices you have learned to heal the deepest parts of your heart.

PROTECTOR OF LOVE #2: TRUTH

In Kundalini yoga we say *sat nam,* a Sanskrit salutation. It is woven into the mantras and chants that we sing and repeat as part of the yoga practice itself. The translation is "truth is my name." I have been intrigued by the message of *sat nam* for as long as I have practiced Kundalini yoga. At some level it seems like a given: of course I want to honor the truth of who I am! But before cultivating this practice of awareness, I so often did not really relate to the truth of who I was.

We can think of truth as it relates to others, as being honest, doing what we say we will do, doing business with respect, clarity, and full disclosure—basically, doing the right thing. The value there is incredible, but what does it look like to tap into the truth of *who you are* and *how you relate to yourself in truth*? That can be trickier than it seems. For example, how often do you compromise your feelings for another person because having the tough conversation is just too hard? What does your heart feel like when you stay in an environment where there is abuse, upset, or disrespect? How truthful are you about the sources of stress in your life? What does it feel like to move ahead when your energy has indicated your exhaustion? Are you honoring truth of self then?

The connection of personal truth to self-healing and self-love is often overlooked. Either we are not connected to the experience in front of us or we have actively made a decision to override and move beyond the information out of convenience despite the important messages within. When we overlook our relationship with the heart, we miss out on the vital messages of personal truth. We have not paid attention to the personal truth inside of us. This disconnection starts to affect all of the Four Elements. But worse still is that we have lost the heart's trust, and in losing that trust we start believing the untruthful stories of the ego. Now is the time to reconnect to your heart in truth.

PROTECTOR OF LOVE #3: GRATITUDE

There is no faster way to turn life's hurtful events around than to find gratitude in the tiniest pockets of life right here, right now. It is an easy out to say, "There is nothing in my life to be grateful for." This lazy sentiment harms the heart enormously. When we fall back into the patterns of discouragement and victimhood of the past, we can feel ourselves sinking deeper into that which separates us from the love of the heart. To feel our connection to the heart, we must believe in the heart's ability to turn things around for us when we sink into sorrow. Being grateful does this: it puts the discomfort of hurt aside and says, "I understand your hurt, but that is just one slice of the pie in your outrageously wonderful life. Now let's give gratitude for the rest." Gratitude doesn't allow us to pull the curtain on life and resign ourselves to misery and defeat. The heart is always looking for something or someone to give gratitude to, and when we cut ourselves off from that opportunity, we suffer greatly.

Gratitude serves in extraordinary ways. It showers us in appreciation for our courage to step away from difficulty with grace and allows us to witness that same courage and grace in those around us. Appreciation serves as a bolster to life's disturbances. We build the strength to see the positive, even though all we might see in a moment of pain are shades of gray. Gratitude elevates our energy from the depths of sadness and lifts us up to see the good that exists, even in the gloomiest of times.

Gratitude illuminates your spirit and will draw others to you too. Get in the habit of continually practicing gratitude. Be grateful for the obvious, like the sun and moon rising and setting, the rain that falls to hydrate the earth, and also for the not so obvious events of your life, like a hard lesson learned or the knowledge revealed to you as a result of a physical disability. Offer gratitude to as much in your life as you can, and watch how happy it makes your heart.

PROTECTOR OF LOVE #4: BRAVERY

Every time we take a step in the direction of love, we become the guardian of the heart's energy. In your life, that might mean forgiving yourself for a hurtful act or expressing forgiveness for someone else's hurtful act. Knowing when your heart is suffering and when it is thriving allows you to take calm, mindful action in reaction to what shows up in your life.

In my life, I have become aware of the difference between the energy of my heart and the actions of my ego. I know that when I am ignited, angry, and reactive, I am working from my untrained mind, the ego, and I do my best to step away until I can calm down and reconnect to my heart. To make a decision in the heat of an angry moment will only bring further harm to your heart and the hearts of others involved. It is unconscious acts that do the most harm to us and to those we strike out against. Similarly, taking on coping methods to manage the disorder instead of finding ways to move through it can cause further damage.

Stepping away is an act of bravery and great service. But love doesn't always show up wrapped in a box with a bow on it. Sometimes it is delivered to us through suffering or through a confrontation with someone we love deeply. This is where bravery comes in. It takes great courage to recognize when you are suffering, and even more courage to do something about it. It is a natural instinct to want to strike out against whatever it might be that hurts you, but a healing choice steps forth from strength and love.

Offering love as a response is transformative. Love heals the heart. The heart takes note of your efforts that move you closer to love, and over time, it gets stronger. It begins, once again, to trust your actions. Without this heart connection, our actions originate from an untrained mind and will always have an ego-based reaction. Think of your love connection as the engine for all the good you will do in the world. Forgiveness is a courageous and powerful act, and it will impact your life in huge ways.

PROTECTOR OF LOVE #5:
MUTUALLY LOVING RELATIONSHIPS

In this chapter we've been looking at what helps the heart find strength and preserves it from being torn down, overlooked, and defeated. Heart health is about establishing a relationship with your heart that is sound and dependable. This relationship assures you that you will consider your heart first, and from that trust of heart you will move safely and love freely. Giving and receiving is a measuring stick of that movement.

It is no mystery how uncomfortable it can feel to be the only one giving in a relationship. The energy gets disturbed rapidly, and soon all sorts of emotions show up to warn us that the scales have been tipped. This can ignite anger and resentment easily, so pay attention when this happens before things unwind too far. Whether it is giving too much or taking too much, the outcome can feel similar: both rob the giver and the recipient of a meaningful, balanced connection.

The heart longs for connection, interaction, and the chance to tap into pure love. In my experience, giving is far easier than receiving. Giving can soothe our own personal wounds, or it can be manipulative, something that makes us feel better about ourselves—at least for a little while. Excessive giving is destructive and builds a false reputation to make up for a damaged sense of self.

Those who more easily take love than give love may be so beaten down that there is nothing to give. They can only take, and it's never enough to make them feel whole. Like any coping mechanism, it ends up doing more damage than good. It's less about the other person and more about distracting yourself from being honest about the pain in your life.

When we come from a state of balance, we can create incredible bonds of love and support that effortlessly flow. When we give, we have the opportunity to feel ourselves move out of our comfort zone and extend ourselves in loving ways. When we easily receive and share our own gifts in return, we honor ourselves, believing wholeheartedly that we are worthy of other people's time, energy, and love.

TRUSTING YOUR HEART

After pain, it takes great courage to come back to a place of trust. When you have been hurt, believing that *this time* will be different is a leap of faith. But what I have found over and over again is that when I weigh the possibilities of trust against the limitations of fear, trust wins every time. Fear is a dead end street. Trust opens our lives to a bright future, one filled with hope and love and one that supports the growth of trust in our hearts.

Identifying emotions in your life is empowering. When you know what you feel and why you feel that way, you can choose which people, places, and things you want to have in your life. You can stand witness to the situations that bring on fear, self-doubt, and negativity, learn from them, and move on. Remember: every situation can be changed, and nothing is without hope.

Becoming aware of how happiness feels in your body and what brings you happiness turns you into a happiness magnet. Positivity will begin to appear. Even if these moments are fleeting at first, you will start to feel yourself more attracted to what feels right and less to what doesn't. You will start noticing patterns of communication and behavior that bring on suffering and you will ask yourself, "Why do I keep repeating this behavior?" You'll know in advance that your buttons are being pushed, and you will prepare yourself by saying, "I am aware of my sensitivities and I will pay extra attention to my reactions." Learning your emotional boundaries is important. It is always okay to take a time out from a situation by saying, "I need some air. I'm uncomfortable, and I want to gather my thoughts." Know when to get off the phone, leave the room, or take a walk around the block. This is the Stop, Look, and Listen technique that we talked about on page 102. Revisit these exercises and notice the benefits they bring to your life.

As you get to know yourself more and more from the inside, you'll have the chance to trust what comes up. You'll start to rely on the messages of the heart rather than being guided by the ego's fear. You will come into relationship with what feels really good, and you'll appreciate it like you never have before. This reconnection will make you feel alive again. You won't be on the fence wondering what could really make you feel happy—you'll know!

chapter 11

The Spirit

A strong, balanced spirit has the unique ability to trust the unknown, invisible, and intangible. Spirit is the ultimate believer. It can be more powerful in action than any of the other Four Elements of Human Life. When you depend upon spirit, it shows up and teaches you how to move out of fear and into faith. When we build a connection to the spirit, we remember what it feels like to be held. We understand what it is like to be in partnership. We access the knowledge of heaven and earth. Through relationship with the spirit, we have the chance to draw on knowledge that is otherwise not readily available to us.

The spirit is the part of us that is revealed as we practice self-care and cultivate self-love. Spirit lives in that self-love. It is responsive to the deepest parts of our being. Its guidance is powerful yet effortlessly administered when we hold faith. We can let go of the need to know everything and micromanage our lives in exhausting ways. In faith we can see the big-picture successes, guided by a divine force. We can let go of coping mechanisms and unhealthy attachments like the negative storylines of the mind. The release of the ego's manipulations frees us to be in the loving, honest presence of the spirit.

This chapter is the culmination of all your efforts so far. You have built a foundation strong enough to hold your spirit. Celebrate your efforts and trust the extraordinary energy you have cultivated to get you to this point. You have paved the way for marvelous things to happen, and now you are ready to experience your spirit in whatever way it shows up to be healed. When you're ready to listen, the spirit's guidance is always there for you. All you have to do is believe.

DISCONNECTING FROM THE SPIRIT

I have seen friends and clients fall victim to upheaval in their lives because they feel there is no other choice. Living on the edge, with lots of risk and drama, can be exciting at first. These highs and lows can seduce us into feeling exhilarated, and living without that sort of conflict feels boring. But soon you realize how tiring it is to maintain that level of drama in your life. It can be confusing for those of us who grew up in unsettled circumstances. If you were raised in a home where there was financial instability, neglect, abandonment, abuse, or lack of support, it can feel normal and natural to keep on seeking upheaval in your adult life. Awareness around your circumstances will help you understand that a high-drama life is not normal and will wear you down.

What does all this have to do with the spirit? Everything. The person living that high-drama life is out of touch with her spirit. She burns bridges, makes snap judgments, and doesn't know which way to turn. She can't access that calm, quiet place inside that trusts deeply. Why does this happen? Maybe selfish or self-sabotaging instincts are getting the better of her and telling her to ignore the spirit for a while.

Living at the mercy of your impulses is an ego-driven way of being that shuts out the wisdom of the spirit. Extreme highs and lows, competition, jealousy, and backstabbing do not lay a foundation for the spirit to flourish. The joy of the spirit retreats. Instead, the spirit is actively trying to wake us. We feel suffering strongly. We overreact to the pain of uncertainty by rejecting responsibility, causing disappointment and hurting others. These warning signs are the spirit urging us to notice how uncomfortable and out of balance we are in this ego-driven life.

It is from this discomfort that we can take steps to change and realign ourselves with spirit once again.

Or maybe the culprit is apathy, a state of numb indifference, a sort of uninvestigated dissatisfaction that eliminates our motivation to grow our spirit. It's a low-lying hum of sadness that is ever-present, infiltrating the way you feel every minute of every day. Apathy causes you to numb yourself from what is most uncomfortable instead of learning from the pain and making changes. Apathy doesn't change the reality of your life. It just gives you permission to disregard that reality.

When we close ourselves off from the wisdom of the spirit, we lose our best resource and guide. Life is void of what is most precious, invigorating, and reaffirming. We suffer mood swings and a broken heart. We make bad decisions that have damaging effects on all Four Elements. Life is torn up in fear, anxiety, resentment, and hatred as a result of closing out the flow of your spirit.

SPIRIT PRACTICE #1:
THE SENSITIVITY SCALE

Emotions are a function of the heart, but the intensity with which you feel them has a lot to do with the spirit. When dealing with the tough stuff in life, emotions can peak in intensity and can be difficult to deal with, which is why the numbness of apathy can be so appealing. But don't be afraid of strong emotions. They are an expression of a powerful spirit, and they function to ignite us into action.

This exercise is designed to help open us up to a stronger connection with the spirit. What's involved is simply to observe your engagement with your own emotions.

— TO DO THE PRACTICE —

Throughout the day, name the emotion you are feeling, and on a scale of one to ten, rate how intense the feeling is for you or how engaged and present you feel, with one being the least and ten being the most. From there, ask yourself, "Am I okay with this level of engagement?" If it's a positive situation, what steps can you take to be more present? If it's a harmful situation, which of this book's self-care practices will help you to find strength again? The exercise prompts you to dialogue with your spirit and empowers you to move through situations. Keep asking questions, and the right answers will appear when you need them.

LISTENING TO THE WHISPERS AND WARNINGS OF THE SPIRIT

Even in a state of apathy, the spirit will try to reach you, to warn you of danger ahead. Some common spirit crises include relationships that aren't working out, the loss of a loved one, and financial situations that threaten your livelihood. These situations can have a major impact on your health and happiness and can be very difficult to change.

How do you know if your spirit is urging you toward change, away from something limiting and toward something expansive? I think of it as whispers and warnings of the spirit. These whispers and warnings can manifest in all sorts of ways. Some people start to feel restless. Others start to pull away from life responsibilities, slacking off or blowing things off, generally showing less effort overall. Sometimes mistakes that you never could have predicted happen, sabotaging your efforts. Many times, the spirit's whispers show up in another of the Four Elements, manifesting as health problems such as mood swings, mental distractions, and sleep issues.

Again, the most important part of healing through these crises is recognizing that they are present in your life to start with. This may sound like a given, but this is where so many of us get stuck. People don't recognize and admit that the symptoms exist in their life; they don't listen to the whispers and warnings of the spirit. Instead they build all sorts of coping mechanisms around their pain and never get to the true source.

Some people are ready to come back into a state of communion with their spirit, while others resist it as much as they can. I understand why—coming back into a place of honest connection with the spirit is the end of old habits that have you lying to yourself. The coping mechanisms, the self-harming decisions, the actions that go against your conscience and your expectations for yourself—those days are over once you start listening to your spirit again.

Don't get me wrong; you can, and will, still do things that you regret. But that's the catch: you will regret them. You will never let yourself get away with that kind of self-sabotage again. When you make the wrong decision or act in a less-than-graceful way, your spirit will whisper its warnings to you in crucial moments. When you trip up, you'll have a different way of measuring what feels right and what feels completely wrong. More than that, you'll want to make it right, and that is the difference, because making it right is where the most valuable learning comes through.

FOLLOWING THE SPIRIT'S GUIDANCE

When we trust the spirit as a guide, we can let go of worry. The spirit's guidance is the most accurate, dependable directional system there is. The spirit is patient and constant, but let there be no mistaking the power the spirit holds. Even when we lose our way, the spirit does not. It is the job of our spirit to shake us up when we fall off the path. It jolts us into remembrance of our purpose here, so we have the chance to set the right course.

It is the prayer of the spirit to have us listen to what needs to be addressed, to stop ignoring the valuable suffering that has arrived to help us grow. Only then can we heal through the most difficult events of life. Even when we lose our way and forget what we came to this earth to do, the spirit always remembers. The spirit knows how good it feels to be aligned with happiness, joy, and laughter. That is where the spirit resides: in the most positive aspects of who we are. When we move toward what makes us happiest, we grow closer to the spirit, the universe, and the world as a whole. The spirit is the ever-present energy that brought us into this world and will usher us out. The spirit's love and faith never leave us, even when it gets masked or muffled.

The spirit is ruthless and diligent in its attempts to wake us up. It wants us to listen so that we can live the best life possible. We all have come here with a purpose. The spirit knows that, and the spirit exists to guide us there. As we try to fulfill that purpose, there are important lessons to learn in this school of life. If you do not succeed in learning the given lesson, it will be given to you again until you succeed.

SPIRIT PRACTICE #2:
ONE HAPPY THING

Clear your mind for a moment and name something that brings you happiness. It can be an experience, person, place, object, idea—the sky's the limit.

This simple exercise just brought you into relationship with your spirit. Any time you spend revisiting something in your life that brings you peace, happiness, joy, and hope, you feel a connection to spirit.

When I did this exercise many years ago, it was easy for me to answer the question: a little knoll on Cape Cod that I liked to visit as a child brought me happiness. But I dismissed my answer as trivial. The spirit is something big, mysterious, and impossible to tap into. I couldn't just summon its wisdom with a snap of the fingers in answer to a simple question. Or could I?

This exercise opened me up to the revolutionary concept that the spirit is everywhere. The spirit can be big, but it can also be found in the tiny moments of life that we often dismiss as insignificant. The spirit can be mysterious, but it can also be familiar. My meditation teacher gave me valuable advice: don't judge your spirit, and don't put expectations on your spirit that make it hard to access. When your spirit speaks to you, listen and let the idea grow.

As I thought about it more, that little knoll represented youthful innocence, security, and a connection to nature—not so trivial after all.

Ask yourself to think of something that brings happiness each day and remember the joyful impression it has on you. Whatever pops up as the answer, honor it. Don't judge it or undermine it. Your spirit supplied that answer at this time and this place for a reason. Keep your energy flowing toward happy places so you can get into the habit of replacing fear with joy.

CONNECTING THE SPIRIT WITH BODY, MIND, AND HEART

The idea of establishing a relationship with your spirit can feel daunting. After all, what does that really mean? Connecting with our spirit means we can better understand the other three elements of being human—the body, heart, and mind—because there is a more immediate relationship to them. Your body is always there, wearing the clothes you picked out, doing the activities you told it to do, sending you information from your five senses. Your mind is present in the thoughts whirling through your consciousness all day. Your heart is there in the highs and lows of your mood, in the pounding of your pulse when you feel excited, in the tears you shed when you feel sad. But how do you feel the spirit's presence?

SPIRIT AND THE BODY

One of the physical ways I relate to my spirit is through the breath. My breath is an indicator of where I am in that moment. It reminds us, when we listen, of the presence of spirit. When we don't access the power of the breath, our breathing is often shallow and pinched and we feel stuck in fearful patterns. On the flipside, we know we are in the healing energy of the spirit when the breath is deep and full. The breath soothes the spirit, which encourages energy to keep flowing and allows us to keep walking through the most challenging of situations.

When we breathe consciously, our relationship with life can be felt in a deeper way. We take our perspective inward and relate to the sensations of the body, mind, and heart through a different lens and we have access to knowledge that we would not otherwise have. What is your spirit saying through your breath?

SPIRIT AND THE MIND

The spirit's influence on the mind is a flowing expression of who we really are. When we let the spirit guide the mind, it does not disappoint us. Spirit is all about the truth. It sees life through a lens of opportunity. There is no obstacle too big or too small. Every situation and circumstance has purpose and life takes on a flowing rhythm. We don't get stuck in the regrets of yesterday and the anxiety of tomorrow. We stay present to what is before us now and move ahead with that information.

The spirit reminds us that we are safe in the moment. When the spirit shines through the mind, we have the opportunity to know ourselves in honesty. We honor our commitments and speak truthfully about what we can do and what we cannot do. The mind is guided by the power of wisdom and intuition. It is no longer enslaved by the overreactions of the imbalanced ego. It is in this place that we intuitively trust that spirit will be generous in offering us endless opportunities to lead a successful, happy life.

Some of the benefits of the union between spirit and mind include:

* Open-mindedness
* An ease and trust of life's course
* Deep faith
* The release of repressed sad feelings
* Seeing life clearly
* A calm, settled mind
* Unity of intuition and intellect
* Profound wisdom

SPIRIT AND THE HEART

Heart energy is spirit energy. When we experience our spirit through the heart, joy becomes the pulse of the spirit. We are not afraid of our emotions; in fact, we long to be connected with our feelings. The spirit wants to feel and express everything we go through. The spirit understands that life is made up of a cycling of all sorts of emotions, so in order to live a rich and full life, we have to be able to feel all of what comes through. Joy, sadness, and everything in between have a part to play in who we are.

Some of the benefits of the union between spirit and heart include:

* Easy reliance on self-care
* Natural awareness of the needs and feelings of others
* Comfort with change
* Ability to adapt to the cycles of life
* Happy, healthy relationships
* Successful routines and disciplines
* Confidence in pursuing our own paths
* Compassion and understanding for different ways of life

SELF-CARE AND THE SPIRIT

When we connect more with our spirit through daily practice, we have the chance to feel what it is like to be a part of something infinite. We no longer live separated from our spirit or the spirits of those around us. We are connected to the whole. We move mountains to grow truth in our lives because we understand that nothing else is more important. I have come to intimately know that true healing cannot happen unless we address the whole of who we are with a strong, steady, disciplined path.

Every act of self-care is a nourishing gesture for the spirit, and just like any relationship, the more time we spend caring for it, the more it flourishes. When we fortify our relationship with the spirit, we show up as a dedicated, loving friend to ourselves. Through discipline we are able to trust our spirit and it becomes an active part of our life. The spirit no longer has to take dramatic measures to wake us up; we are awake. Now the spirit can do what it does best—bring us faith, love, and an unfaltering trust in that place of peace that resides within.

Meditation, self-care, self-love, and self-healing are potent tools for connecting with and cultivating our spirit. In short, we are making time for the most essential part of who we are. As the famous French Philosopher Pierre Teilhard de Chardin put it, "We are not human beings having a spiritual experience. We are spiritual beings having a human experience." As you move closer to your true self, your spirit will be your constant, steady friend. It will never leave you, and fear will continue to fall away while your faith grows. The real magnificence of the spirit appears in the quiet, prayerful moments of your life, in nature, in heartfelt conversations, and in times of compassion and forgiveness. It is in those times that you will feel most alive in spirit.

SPIRIT PRACTICE #3:
SPIRITUAL SAVINGS ACCOUNT

Think of your spirit as a bank account. The size and security of your bank account goes a long way to contributing to your life. The larger your bank account, the fewer your worries. You have your essentials covered, and you're even ready for an unforeseen large expense and withdrawal. Likewise, the smaller the bank account gets and the bigger the withdrawals, the more you are heading for trouble. When your bank account has reached its limit and goes into negative balance, it is a true emergency.

Now think of your spirit as the bank account, and your energy as the currency. When you make frequent deposits into your spiritual savings account through self-care, meditation, and other activities that bring you joy, you have plenty of currency in your account to handle the unexpected withdrawals from this energetic savings account. Pay attention to the quality and amount of energy you deposit into your spiritual savings account. Notice how much stronger life feels when there is abundant currency in the account.

What do deposits into the spiritual bank account look like? Adding restorative practices to our lives that help us keep a steady perspective and give us the strength to flourish through all times. You are in charge of this energy, so get clear about what fills you up and what depletes you, continuously building on your energetic foundation so you can access what you need in challenging times.

Examples of spiritual savings account deposits:

* Eat wholesome, delicious, fresh foods
* Visit an art museum
* Go somewhere in your hometown that you've never visited before
* Wear your favorite color
* Make or buy an impromptu gift for someone you love
* Write a kind letter to someone you miss
* Join a club or volunteer group
* Go to the library or bookstore and pick out a book outside of your usual interests
* Spend time with the elderly at your local retirement home or senior center
* Volunteer for a few hours at your local animal shelter
* Make a recipe you've always wanted to try

I started using this practice in my life shortly after I started to meditate. Life began to feel more roomy very fast. I found myself less reactive and more capable of generosity in how I dealt with my own life. Instead of being filled to the brim with dread, sadness, and anger, my spiritual bank account was full and I was becoming a storehouse for positive, healing energy. Which simple pleasures would you like to put into your spiritual savings account?

FINDING SPONTANEOUS INSPIRATION

When we live in relationship to the spirit, we tap into a mystical, magical part of our being. For anyone who has experienced this connection, you know what I mean. Through your self-care practices, your spirit flourishes. One of the most powerful gifts of a robust spirit is spontaneous inspiration.

Spontaneous inspiration is a flash of knowledge that pops into your head. You are not sure where it came from because it feels different from your normal way of thinking. It is larger, more inclusive, and infinitely wiser than the finite thought patterns of the mind. It feels intriguing, so you go along with it...and then something amazing happens. Maybe you end up in the right place at the right time or you are blessed with good fortune, or you cross paths with someone who changes your life forever. Spontaneous inspiration opens up space in your life to invite fate in. If this sounds far out, let's get grounded about it. We've all had experiences of spontaneous inspiration. It can be the impulse to take the scenic route home and finding out later that you missed terrible traffic or even an accident. Maybe you get drawn down a certain aisle at the bookstore and you end up finding a book that blows you away (maybe even this book!). Maybe it's the bright idea that turned into a new business opportunity. Or the impulse to go to that party or reunion, even though it was out of your comfort zone, and you meet the love of your life there. These things can happen to anyone, but when you add self-care practices, you tap into spontaneous inspiration all the time.

If it weren't for spontaneous inspiration, this book would not exist. In 2013, I had wrapped up a long-running yoga program and was taking a little downtime before gearing up for the next phase in my career. I bumped into an acquaintance at a coffee shop one day, and she asked me what I was going to do next. I had been asking myself the same question for weeks, as had my family and colleagues. For whatever reason, at that moment the answer popped into my head and out of my mouth: "It's time for me to write a book." I started writing that very day and never looked back.

FUELING THE SPIRIT WITH FAITH

When we make the decision to add nurturing self-care practices to our lives, it takes discipline to keep up with them. To do so, we need to train our brains away from old habits and toward ways of being that heal, grow, and connect us to the spirit. This means setting up a sacred space with consideration and love, maintaining consistent yoga and meditation, and mastering breath. Discipline builds the foundation of a life that can flourish. We have given ourselves the chance to come into direct relationship with the eternal part of who we are—the spirit—and to follow a path to our purpose here on earth. We have experienced the positive shifts that daily practice brings to us, and now we can let go of skepticism and come into faith. When we believe, we set ourselves on a powerful path that does not rely on the outer circumstances of life.

As you move forward, you'll transform discipline—the repetition of these practices to learn a new way of being—into an effortless and joyful devotional life practice. Your practice becomes more than a set of rules, it is something you cannot live without. Now is the time to have faith in what you have created—that faith-filled path can be thought of as a devotional path. Devotional self-care lands us in the present moment, the place where spirit is most alive in us. We have elevated our energy through our daily discipline and believe in something far greater than the temporary conditions of the past. Now we have faith in what appears in the moment, and we devote ourselves to that learning.

This devotion is not necessarily a religious faith but a direct line to the spirit that can align with any religion or spiritual practice that is part of who you are. It's a feeling of trust in the unknown, the part of life you can't see, feel, or touch. You can call it God, Spirit, or the Universe, whatever helps you find that part of yourself that so often gets lost in the busyness of life. When you come back to your practice day after day, you become more and more inspired by your spirit and faith and spirit become one. This harvest of the spirit offers a strong sense of self and a tender awareness of the interconnectedness of your body, mind, and heart.

When your faith and spirit are strong, you see life differently. You notice people, situations, and the environment in a whole new way. Everything is possible when you are strong enough to live with truth and integrity, to seek out joy and to have faith in your own wisdom. Rather than run from a challenge, you stand before it in all your strength and ask for your lessons to be revealed to you. You are ready to heal and grow.

Sitting at the Feet of Your Life

You have come so far on your journey and your progress will be there for you for the rest of your precious life. You have said a resounding yes to your life. May the road always stay open for you to travel on.

It is an honor to meet a guru, saint, or blessed person, and even to be worthy to sit by their feet. You are a student, showing respect to the greatness and grace that person has achieved. Likewise, by welcoming you into their presence, the blessed person honors you. This kind of revered relationship is how you should look at your life. The whole, long, intense experience, with every up and every down, deserves the utmost gratitude and respect. Sitting at the feet of your life means experiencing the lessons and blessings of this extraordinary life. When you lay your head down for the final time, you will have the honor of looking back on your life and knowing that you did everything possible to make the most of your time here on earth. It is the ultimate honor. You surrendered, accepted, and now feel completely grateful.

Anytime the road starts to get bumpy and you begin to feel like you are running on fumes, remember that every time we do something that is nurturing for ourselves, we fill the tank. We put energy into our lives instead of taking it out. Self-care can be taken for granted until a difficult life event happens that threatens your happiness or possibly your survival. This is when you pray that the tank is full enough to deal with what shows up because when the tank is empty, life becomes fragile, shaky, and undependable. Suddenly your self-care becomes your lifeline. You completely depend on your routines and rituals to sustain you. You access these practices and rely on them as your best friend and confidant to steer and guide you to safety. You have found freedom to be in the moment without the dread of waiting for the inevitable discomfort of change to happen. I transition in life more gently now because my tank is continually being filled by the self-love, self-care, and meditation practices I have committed to in my life.

You stand before your life like a strong tree, roots deep in the ground, trunk and limbs powerful yet flexible, moving with the ever-changing events of life. You understand your life more clearly now because of the foundation you have built, and opportunities for further growth are open-ended. You have seen results and felt emotions that were shut down long ago. You are now interacting with your life in a way that you never truly dreamed possible. The lights of your life are shining bright because of your hard work and your commitment to your path. The wonder of it all is that nothing and nobody will ever be able to take this self-knowledge away from you. You have opened doors that cannot be closed again. Your consciousness has expanded, and you now have an understanding of who you are in the world and what you can accomplish. Whatever path you choose at this point, you will move forward with new knowledge of yourself that will be yours forever. You know yourself in a different way now, and your path will be illuminated in exactly the way it needs to be revealed to you. Utilize what you can and strive to be loving on your path of self-discovery. Your compass is accurate and always pointed home to your heart. So stay steady, trust your path, and enjoy the ride, because all paths now lead you home.

LIST OF PRACTICES

ACKNOWLEDGMENTS

I have deep respect for what it takes to create anything. And I have learned from this project that the best creative expressions come from collaboration. As I sit here today, I am humbled by the two and half years that it has taken to write this book and all the people who showed up to help make it happen.

Inside has been brewing in me for a very long time. Although I am completely self-taught, with no formal degree in writing, I feel I was born to write this book. In many ways this has been accomplished through a lifetime of journaling.

All of the lessons I needed to learn to heal the sadness and quell the fears I experienced from the loss of my mother and father had to be experienced before I could write a book on healing. Deep loss and fear bring on angry emotions when they are not heard and listened to, and I was a very angry, hurt person for a long time. I pay tribute to Dr. Roger Lamora for helping me make sense of a life that felt so disconnected and discouraging. His wise and brilliant knowledge of trauma and abandonment helped me find the balance and boundaries needed to create a life worth living.

As I gained strength and awareness, incredible teachers and guides showed up to help me learn about something greater than what meets the eye. I learned about God, the Universe, and Nature and embraced them as a part of who I am. My love of life was influenced by the knowledge and wisdom they felt was important enough to pass on; I was one of the fortunate ones to sit at the feet of this learning.

Ralph Lucier is my longtime friend and business partner. He is the design brilliance behind all of my branding. He created my logo when I began my massage practice in 1991 and has been the force behind all of the design that has my name on it. He gets me, and this is a huge thing when so much of what I dream to express is intangible. Ralph, you are a cheerleader and inspiration to me, and my work would not know the degree of success it knows without you.

Alexandra Winslow was my editor and social media expert for the first part of this project. We worked together closely for a year and a half. As a first-time author, very simple concepts eluded me. Alexandra was the organizing force behind me. She held my hand, giving me guidance and instruction in a way that I could always hear. She taught me clarity and the power of simplicity in writing about a topic so intimidating: trauma. I reflect on our time together warmly.

Leda Scheintaub is the editor who helped me complete this book. Leda's knowledge of editing is astounding. The project needed fresh eyes, and Leda's eyes were the ones I needed. Leda not only had the editing experience, but as a Kundalini yogi she also understood the yogic aspects of the book. It is hard to hand off a manuscript that has so much personal meaning in it; Leda gave me the encouragement and support to do this easily. Leda, I thank you for your efficiency and grace in bringing my words to life. I hope that this is the first of many projects we work on together.

As a first time author, I depended on the generosity of others for guidance. This can be a lot to ask of professionals who have their own demanding schedules. Terry Walters has continually opened her arms to me. She offered me her resources, found time to read and endorse my book, and in shaky times infused her vast knowledge of writing to help me keep on. Terry, thank you for your belief in my book. I will pass forward your kindness.

Eric Brassard, my son, is a man with abundant knowledge of media, writing, and life. His career experience as a TV executive in Los Angeles has supplied this project with boundless resources. He also knows his mother and has the ability to dance between the personal and professional seamlessly. Eric, thank you for making yourself available to me when I needed guidance as a writer and moral support as a person. It has been a dear experience to share this book project with you.

To my daughter, Alexa, who advised me in critical times. Her influence on my writing has steered the direction of the book. Alexa, thank you for helping me to understand that people in emotionally fragile places need a simple guide to follow.

None of this book project would have been possible without my husband, David. He has believed in me from the beginning. He attended Kundalini yoga classes to support me as a teacher, even when it really wasn't his thing. He embraced a ten-month Kundalini yoga training in the barn on our property and encouraged me through ten years of teaching Kundalini classes in the barn. I took a sabbatical to write this book with his blessing. David, I am so fortunate for all you have brought to my life.

To my brothers and sisters, I have no words for what you mean to me. We have traveled together for a long time. Thank you for your unwavering love and protective arms.

I am in this life because of my parents. I love you both now and forever. We do the best we can with the circumstances given to us, and with all my heart, I know you did your best.

Index